EXPLORING DEBATE 2

Jack Clancy　　**Sean Bienert**

contents

Book 2

Is it fair that some people have an advantage getting into college?

UNIT 01	School Uniforms	... 5
UNIT 02	Cell Phones	... 11
UNIT 03	College	... 17
UNIT 04	File Sharing	... 23

Should I go to college?

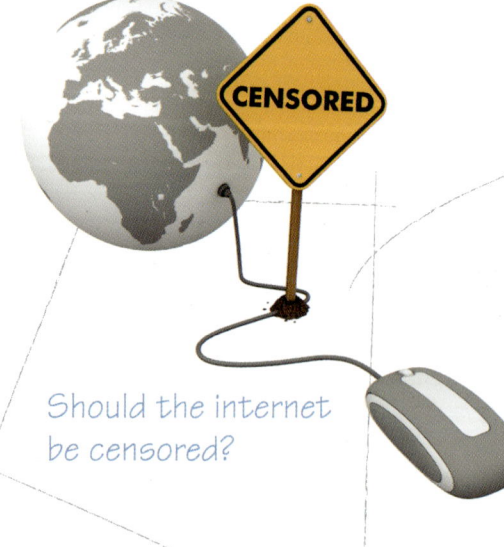

Should the internet be censored?

UNIT 05	Internet Censorship	... 29
UNIT 06	CCTV	... 35
UNIT 07	Privacy of Public Figures	... 41
UNIT 08	Fashion	... 47

UNIT 09	Advertisement ... 53
UNIT 10	Legacy Preference ... 59
UNIT 11	Cloning ... 65
UNIT 12	Death Penalty ... 71

Should the death penalty be allowed?

UNIT 13	Abortion ... 77
UNIT 14	Arranged Marriage ... 83
UNIT 15	Social Networking ... 89
UNIT 16	Zoos ... 95

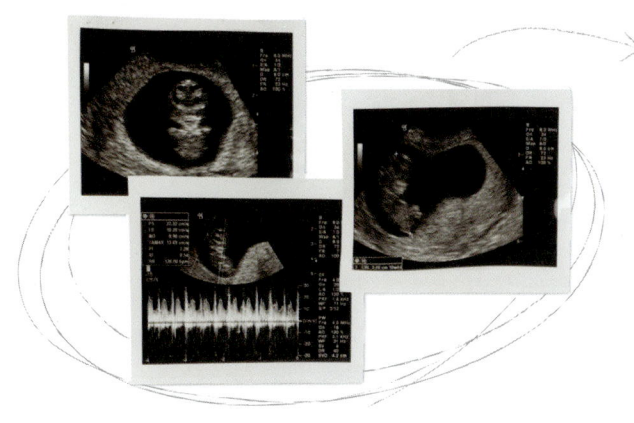

Is a fetus a human being?

UNIT 17	Single Sex vs. Coed ... 101
UNIT 18	Space Exploration ... 107
UNIT 19	Free Trade Agreements (FTAs) ... 113
UNIT 20	Human Nature... Good or Evil? ... 119

Is human nature good or evil?

School Uniforms

Warm-up

- Fill in each job box with a different job that requires workers to wear a uniform. Then fill in different pieces of the uniform in the box below it.

Police Officer		
whistle		
bulletproof vest		
good boots for running		
taser or pepper spray		

- Interview a classmate using the questions below.

  1. Do you like wearing uniforms? Why or why not?
  2. What do your parents think about school uniforms?

School Uniforms

🟠 Read the passage.

Track 1

Uniforms are everywhere. Your parents may wear them at work. Sports players wear them to show that they are part of a team. Others wear them to look professional. But should children wear uniforms in schools?

Many people believe that wearing school uniforms will make children better students. They will focus more on work and not on the clothes their friends are wearing. Everyone will be equal and it will eliminate the feeling of competition to impress friends. Children will be happier and work harder. They will also have more school spirit.

Uniforms can also decrease negative behavior and violence in students. Students are often teased because of the clothes they wear. Certain groups wear similar clothes and isolate those who look different. Uniforms make everyone the same. Students will be judged by who they are, not by what they wear.

Opponents of uniforms believe that uniforms can suppress a student's individuality. Uniforms force everyone to be the same. Being unique is very important for children, especially teenagers. They want to try new things and impress their friends. If they are forced to conform it may be bad for their development. Other students may not feel comfortable in their uniforms. If they are not comfortable and confident they may perform poorly in class. Uniforms can also be expensive, which is difficult for the parents.

Comprehension Check   Answer the questions.

1. How do school uniforms affect parents?
2. How can school uniforms eliminate the feeling of competition between students?
3. What do opponents of school uniforms believe?
4. What can happen to a student who is not comfortable in the school uniform?
5. Why are children often teased in school?

Vocabulary Check   Complete the sentence with a word from the box.

| unique | teased | eliminate | development | conformed |

1. I want to find a cure to _____ cancer.
2. I did what my mom told me to do, and I _____ to her rules.
3. James _____ me because I did not know the answer.
4. Reading is so important for children's mental _____.
5. I only saw one purple dog. It was _____.

Think About It

Think about the advantages and disadvantages of wearing a school uniform.

Advantages
- Decreases negative behavior and violence in students
-
-

Disadvantages
- Students are not allowed to express themselves with their clothes.
-
-

Opinion Practice

- **Practice supporting/refuting the opinions.**

Supporting Opinions

1. School uniforms are boring... _____
2. Students should be allowed to express themselves... _____
3. Schools should make students wear uniforms... _____
4. Children should wear the most popular clothes... _____

> a. because everyone is the same. Variety is more exciting.
>
> b. since expressing yourself helps you develop as a person.
>
> c. because other people will think they are cool.
>
> d. because it increases a student's performance in school and decreases violence.

Refuting Opinions

1. If students have to wear uniforms then teachers should, too. _____
2. It is important for everyone to be equal in school. _____
3. School uniforms are too expensive. _____
4. Students who wear a uniform are smarter than other students. _____

> a. That's not true. It is cheaper to buy school uniforms. Popular clothes are more expensive.
>
> b. I disagree. Uniforms are for students. Teachers are not the same as students, so they do not need a uniform.
>
> c. No, it is more important for students to be unique. Being different is a good thing.
>
> d. That's not necessarily true. The clothes you wear don't make you smart. If you study hard you will be smart.

Opinion Examples

● **Read the opinions and answer the questions.**

Track 2

❝ I think that there should be no school uniforms. For one thing, buying uniforms is very expensive for my parents. They must buy all of the outfits I need for school, and I still need clothes for when I am not in school. Also, I don't like my uniform. It is ugly and I feel uncomfortable wearing it. I would be happier at school if I could wear the clothes that I like. My parents would be happy, too, because they would save money. ❞

Opinion B

Track 3

❝ I think that students should wear school uniforms. Firstly, it would be cheaper for parents. Without a uniform, students would need many different outfits. They would also need cool, new outfits, which are very expensive to buy. Secondly, students who do not dress cool would be teased and made to feel isolated. It is too much pressure for students to worry about their clothes. Uniforms would make students happier, and the parents would save money, too. ❞

1. Please circle the main idea in each opinion.

2. Please underline the supporting ideas in each opinion.

3. What could you say to further support the opinion with which you agree?

Discussion Questions

● **Discuss the questions in groups.**

1. Adults often wear uniforms when they work. Do you think that wearing a uniform in school will prepare students for work in the future?

2. Should students be allowed to decide if they want to wear uniforms?

3. Some children are mean and violent. Do you think that they will be less mean and violent if they are wearing a school uniform?

4. Many students do not wear their school uniform properly. Teachers are often forced to correct these children. What is the best way to solve this problem?

5. Parents should always buy their children the best, new clothes. Their children need to have the newest fashion to fit in at school. Do you agree with this statement?

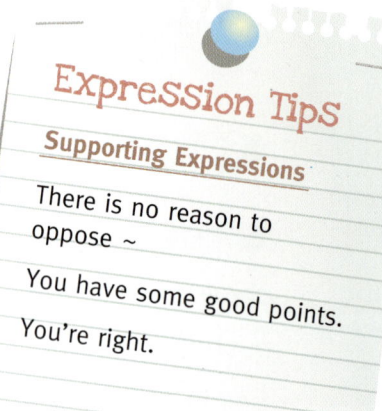

Expression Tips
Supporting Expressions
There is no reason to oppose ~
You have some good points.
You're right.

Time to Debate

Choose one statement. Debate the statement in groups.
(One group agrees with the statement, the other group disagree with the statement.)

1. Parents and teachers worry too much about the clothes that children wear. Children are just expressing themselves. They should be allowed to wear whatever they want.

2. In the future all schools will require students to wear uniforms.

3. Wearing a school uniform will increase school spirit. It will make you proud to belong to your school.

UNIT 2 Cell Phones

Warm-up

● Match these people with the reasons you would call them.

People	Reason to call
1. Police officer	a. You are feeling sick and need medicine.
2. Fire fighter	b. Your dog is sick.
3. Doctor	c. You see that your neighbor's car is on fire.
4. Classmate	d. Someone is being robbed and needs help.
5. Veterinarian	e. You forgot your homework assignment and need to know what it is.

● Interview a classmate using the questions below.

1. Do you have a cell phone? Explain why or why not.
2. Do your parents have cell phones? What do they use them for?

Cell Phones

○ **Read the passage.**

Cell phones are a relatively new invention. They were created in the 1970s, and today there are more than 4 billion cell phones in use worldwide. Most people own a cell phone, but should you?

Today it is very easy to talk to people. Thanks to cell phones we can call people whenever we want, wherever we are. If there is an emergency, we can call for help. If we are lost, we can call for directions. We can keep in touch with family and friends while we are away from home. Parents can keep track of their children, which helps to keep kids safe. Newer cell phones also allow us to play games, use the internet, send and receive text messages, and take pictures.

Cell phones are not perfect. Car accidents and other injuries have been attributed to people using cell phones while driving. Cell phones emit radiation, which some scientists believe can lead to brain tumors or cancer. It can also be expensive to own cell phones. Monthly fees often exceed $100. Some people become addicted and spend too much time using their phones. Sometimes it is a good thing for people not to know where you are. Children may also misuse their cell phones and get into trouble.

Cell phones are still new, and it is difficult to predict what their long-term effects will be. We must continue to study how cell phones affect our safety and health.

Comprehension Check Answer the questions.

1. What has been attributed to people using cell phones while driving?
2. When were cell phones created?
3. Why is radiation dangerous?
4. How many cell phones are in use today?
5. What can we do with new cell phones?

Vocabulary Check Complete the sentence with a word from the box.

keep in touch	relatively	radiation	attributed	billion

1. There are more than 7 _____ people on Earth.
2. Good health is _____ to good diet and exercise.
3. Gamma rays are a kind of _____ which is harmful to humans.
4. When I travel, I try to _____ with my family.
5. A dog is _____ small when compared to an elephant.

Think About It

Think about the advantages and disadvantages of cell phones.

Advantages
- Some cell phones let us use the internet.
-
-

Disadvantages
- Can cause car accidents and other injuries
-
-

13

Opinion Practice

● **Practice supporting/refuting the opinions.**

Supporting Opinions

1. Parents should give their children cell phones... _____
2. Teachers should ban cell phones from school... _____
3. Cell phones will make you sick... _____
4. Drivers should not be allowed to use cell phones... _____

> a. because students should focus on learning at school, not on talking to friends.
>
> b. since they use radiation which is not safe for humans.
>
> c. because they are a big distraction and can lead to an accident.
>
> d. because their children will be safer if there is an emergency.

Refuting Opinions

1. Car accidents are caused by bad drivers, not cell phones. _____
2. You should stop using cell phones because they cause brain tumors. _____
3. Cell phones are too expensive; home phones are cheaper. _____
4. Children should have cell phones because they will learn to be responsible. _____

> a. It all depends on the plan that you pay for. Many cell phones allow you to call certain people or text for free.
>
> b. Cell phones are toys for children. They will use them to play games and talk to friends, not to learn about responsibility.
>
> c. That's not true. Cell phones distract drivers. If they are not paying attention, an accident can happen.
>
> d. That's not necessarily true. Doctors are still not sure if using cell phones makes you sick. You may not get sick at all.

Opinion Examples

● Read the opinions and answer the questions.

Track 5

❝ I love my cell phone! I can talk to all of my friends whenever I want. I can call my parents if I am in trouble. I can call the police if there is an emergency. Also, all of my friends have cell phones. It is great to be able to talk to them whenever I want. I feel safe with my cell phone, and I can have fun, too. That's why I think every child should have a cell phone. ❞

Opinion B

Track 6

❝ Children should not have cell phones. All of my classmates have one. They spend more time talking with their friends than anything else. They are less productive in school and spend less time playing sports. One day I was playing soccer with some friends. I asked some classmates if they wanted to play, too. They said "No" because they were too busy texting. They are addicted to their cell phones. It is not allowing them to live normal lives. I do not want that to happen to me. ❞

1. Please circle the main idea in each opinion.
2. Please underline the supporting ideas in each opinion.
3. What could you say to further support the opinion with which you agree?

Discussion Questions

- **Discuss the questions in groups.**

    1. Some cell phones have GPS. This allows other people to know the exact location of your phone anywhere in the world. Is this a good idea?

    2. Some people spend one hour every day using a cell phone. Do you think this is too much time?

    3. Do you think that only adults should be allowed to own a cell phone? Why?

    4. Some people think that cell phones should be banned because they emit radiation. Do you think that cell phones are safe?

    5. Do you think that in the future everyone will own a cell phone? Why or why not?

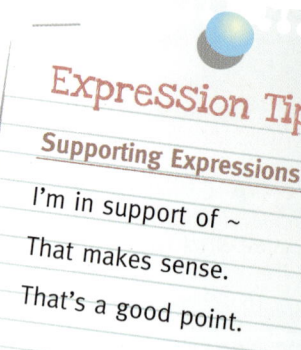

Expression Tips

Supporting Expressions

I'm in support of ~

That makes sense.

That's a good point.

Time to Debate

Choose one statement. Debate the statement in groups.
(One group agrees with the statement, the other group disagree with the statement.)

1. Cell phones should be banned in schools.

2. Cell phones are nice, but people put too much importance on them.

3. Our grandparents did not have cell phones when they grew up. Children today have a much better life because of cell phones.

UNIT 3 College

ED2-03
MP3

Warm-up

- Think of jobs which require a college education. Then think of jobs which you can do without going to college.

Jobs that require college degrees	Jobs that may not require college degrees
doctor,	janitor,

What do you want to be when you grow up? Describe how much education you will need to get this job.

- Interview a classmate using the questions below.

  1. What do you want to be when you grow up? What is your dream job?
  2. Do you want to go to college? Why or why not?

College

🟠 **Read the passage.**

Track 7

Should you go to college? That all depends on what you want to do in life. College is not for everyone, yet many people choose to go. It can prepare us for a great career, or it can be a burden.

Above all else, going to college is an investment in your future. Paying now to get an education means you will be more qualified to get high paying jobs later on. Many careers like those of engineers and lawyers require a lot of studying. There is also a lot of competition for those kinds of jobs. Having a college education can separate you from other applicants because it can prepare you more. You will also get a social education by meeting new people and making job contacts. College professors treat you like an adult and push you to be your best.

But college is not necessary for everyone. It is very expensive. Many people cannot afford it. Taking out student loans can cause financial hardships for you for many years. Many people study for four years, and that is a big commitment. You could spend that time working or travelling. Others go because of family pressure. It would be better to go to college when you know what you want to learn, not because you feel forced to go.

College is a serious decision. You will have to think carefully about what you want to be in the future. Then you can decide if college is the best choice for you.

Comprehension Check Answer the questions.

1. Why do people pay to get a college education?
2. How many years do most people spend studying at college?
3. Why would a college education separate you from others when applying for a job or program?
4. What is a problem with student loans?
5. How can college professors help you?

Vocabulary Check Complete the sentence with a word from the box.

| applicants | qualified | forced | burden | commitment |

1. I didn't want to go to practice, but my friends _____ me to go.
2. He is not _____ to be a judge. He didn't learn how to do it.
3. Many people wanted the new job, so I had to interview many _____.
4. Signing a 5 year contract to play baseball is a big _____.
5. Please don't _____ me with your problems. I have work to do.

Think About It

Think about the advantages and disadvantages of going to college.

Advantages
- Can get better jobs
-
-

Disadvantages
- Four years is a very big commitment.
-
-

Opinion Practice

- **Practice supporting/refuting the opinions.**

Supporting Opinions

1. It is good to travel after high school... _____
2. Parents should make all of their children go to college... _____
3. College is scary... _____
4. Parents should not pressure their children into going to college... _____

> a. because it can be difficult to travel when you have a family and a full time job.
>
> b. because you will be away from your family and friends. The work will be difficult, and there is a lot of pressure to do well.
>
> c. because children should want to go to college. They should not go because they feel like they have to.
>
> d. because it will give their kids the skills they need to get a good job.

Refuting Opinions

1. You should go to college and be a businessman. You will make a lot of money. _____
2. College is a waste of time. You should get a job after high school. _____
3. College is boring. All you do is study. _____
4. College is too expensive. I cannot afford to go. _____

> a. That's not true. You can meet many fun people at college, play sports, play music, and learn about interesting things.
>
> b. No, you should have a job which makes you happy. Go to college only if it helps you to be happy.
>
> c. I disagree. College is an investment in your future. You can get a better job after college.
>
> d. That's not necessarily true. There are many scholarships and loans which can help you pay for college.

Opinion Examples

● Read the opinions and answer the questions.

Track 8

❝ I have to go to college if I want to get a good job. Being rich and successful is very important to me. I want to have a lot of money so that I can support a family and live comfortably. All of the people with the best jobs, like doctors and lawyers, require a college education. Many people want these jobs, too. There is a lot of competition, so I must get the best college education possible. It will separate me from other applicants who are less qualified. ❞

Opinion B

Track 9

❝ I don't need to go to college to get a good job. A college education is a good thing, but not necessary. Many successful people never went to college. Bill Gates is one of the richest men in the world, and he didn't finish college. Many successful athletes and movie stars also did not go to college. I can learn while I work. If I work hard enough I can get a promotion. Or I can start my own business. There are many ways to get a good job. ❞

1. Please circle the main idea in each opinion.
2. Please underline the supporting ideas in each opinion.
3. What could you say to further support the opinion with which you agree?

Discussion Questions

● **Discuss the questions in groups.**

1. Do you think it is better to go to college in your country?

2. Some people go to college when they are adults. Is it better to wait until you're an adult to go to college?

3. Is it important to play sports and do other activities at college, or should you focus all of your energy on studying?

4. Many people let their friends, parents and teachers influence their decisions. Is this a good idea when it comes to going to college?

5. Some people think that studying and taking tests is a bad way to learn. They believe it is better to learn through work experience. Do you think that this is true?

Expression Tips
Refuting Expressions
I am against ~
I cannot accept that ~
I can't agree with your opinion.
I disagree with ~

Choose one statement. Debate the statement in groups.
(One group agrees with the statement, the other group disagree with the statement.)

1. Your parents know what is best for you. If they want you to go to college then you should go.

2. You should study many different things at college. It will make you a more well-rounded person academically. You may also discover new things which you enjoy.

3. College is very expensive. It will take many years to pay your student loans. It would be better to just get a job after high school and save your money.

UNIT 4 File Sharing

Warm-up

- **Fill in the table using the words below.**

Legal to file share	Illegal to file share

personal pictures   episodes of a TV show   poems that you wrote
work files   copyrighted movies   copyrighted computer games
copyrighted mp3s   audio books   pages from copyrighted books
school projects   homework materials   open source files of any type
a song you wrote   music files from an album you bought

- **Interview a classmate using the questions below.**

1. Do you ever download music or movies illegally? Explain why or why not?
2. Do you think it is wrong to download music and movies for free?

File Sharing

🔸 **Read the passage.**

Track 10

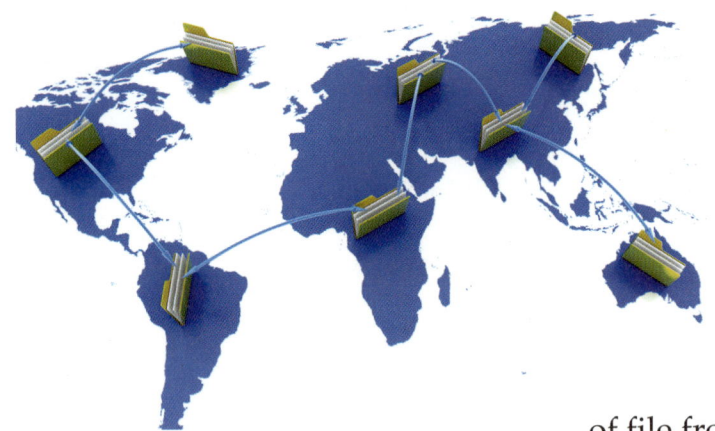

When people think of file sharing they usually think of illegally downloading movies and music. This does happen, and it is a problem, but file sharing can be used for so much more. File sharing is the exchange of any type of file from one person to another using the internet. It can be used for good, but unfortunately is misused.

File sharing is a great system for businesses and schools. You can share files with co-workers and other students easily. It allows you to collaborate on projects even if you are far apart. You can also share pictures with family and friends. New music artists benefit from increased recognition. It is like free publicity as artists do not have to deal with record companies.

Many people also enjoy downloading movies and music for free. In 1999 Napster was the first website to allow free file sharing of music. This is illegal as it violates copyright laws. People caught sharing these files can be arrested.

Many people have been sued and lost a lot of money. Artists also claim that they lose money when people steal their work. Sharing files is also risky. There is a risk of downloading viruses from people you do not know. These viruses can steal your personal information and destroy your computer.

File sharing is a great idea with a lot of potential for the future. Unfortunately, it can be misused and we must be careful to make sure it is used correctly and safely for everyone.

Comprehension Check — Answer the questions.

1. In what year was Napster created?
2. What is file sharing?
3. Why are computer viruses so dangerous?
4. How do artists benefit from file sharing?
5. What can happen to people who are caught illegally downloading files?

Vocabulary Check — Complete the sentence with a word from the box.

| collaborate | recognition | violates | exchange | potential |

1. The two best scientists in the world will _____ on a project to find new forms of energy.
2. You cannot touch the ball with your hands when you play soccer. It _____ the rules.
3. He has the _____ to be a professional baseball player when he grows up.
4. He gained only minimal _____ for his new song.
5. I like your pencil case. Would you like to _____ yours with mine?

Think About It

Think about the advantages and disadvantages of file sharing.

Advantages
- Share pictures with family and friends
-
-

Disadvantages
- There is a temptation to download movies and music illegally.
-
-

Opinion Practice

● **Practice supporting/refuting the opinions.**

Supporting Opinions

1. Artists should like file sharing... _____
2. Teachers should use file sharing in school... _____
3. File sharing is very useful for businesses... _____
4. You should be careful when downloading files from people you don't know... _____

> a. because workers are able to work from home or anywhere they want.
>
> b. because it is a great way for students to work together on projects.
>
> c. because it is free publicity and they can get increased recognition.
>
> d. since they may have viruses which could damage your computer.

Refuting Opinions

1. If you share files with people you do not know you will get a virus. _____
2. If I buy a CD I should be able to share it with all my friends. _____
3. File sharing should be banned because too many people misuse it. _____
4. Children are the ones who misuse file sharing. Parents should teach their children about following the rules. _____

> a. Maybe you are right, but copyright laws make this illegal. If your friends want the CD they must buy it, too.
>
> b. That's not true. Many adults misuse file sharing, too. Everyone needs to learn to follow the rules.
>
> c. I disagree. File sharing has great potential in schools and the workplace. We should simply try to stop people from misusing it.
>
> d. That's not necessarily true. Not all files have a virus, but you still must be careful.

Opinion Examples

- **Read the opinions and answer the questions.**

Opinion A

Track 11

❝ I think that it is wrong to download movies without paying for them. Actors, directors and many other people work very hard to create movies. The same is true for musicians and writers. It is entertainment for us, but it is work for them. Downloading movies is the same as stealing a DVD from a store. Movie companies will lose a lot of money. I would not like it if someone stole from me. We should support our artists by buying their DVDs. ❞

Opinion B

Track 12

❝ I think that it is OK to download movies for free. There are too many new movies today. It is impossible to watch them all because DVDs are very expensive. Going to the cinema is expensive, too. It is also inconvenient. I have to travel to a cinema and watch the movie when they decide to play it. Downloading movies is much easier and cheaper. I can download new and old movies. I can watch them when I want, and many times. I can also watch them from home or on my computer. It is much better this way. ❞

1. Please circle the main idea in each opinion.
2. Please underline the supporting ideas in each opinion.
3. What could you say to further support the opinion with which you agree?

Discussion Questions

● **Discuss the questions in groups.**

1. Would you enjoy collaborating on a class project which involves file sharing?

2. Do you think that the government will ever be able to stop illegal downloading of files?

3. Do you think that movies and CD(DVD)s are too expensive?

4. What do you think is a more dangerous threat, illegal file sharing or computer viruses?

5. Social networking websites like *Facebook* allow you to legally share pictures and files with family and friends. It is a public website, so everyone can look at them, too. Is this a good idea?

Expression Tips
Refuting Expressions
I don't get it.
I don't think ~
I don't think so.

Time to Debate

Choose one statement. Debate the statement in groups.
(One group agrees with the statement, the other group disagree with the statement.)

1. Artists complain too much about illegal file sharing. They should be happy that people want to watch their movies and listen to their music.

2. Many CDs only have one or two good songs. I should not have to pay for eight bad songs when I only want the good ones. If musicians were better I wouldn't have to use file sharing.

3. People who illegally download files should be arrested. It is the same as stealing.

UNIT 5 Internet Censorship

Warm-up

- Fill in the boxes with things that you think might be censored on the internet, and things that might not.

Censored	Not Censored

terrorist recruiting websites   military secrets   bad words
illegal file-sharing websites   illegal pornography   opinions
lies that don't hurt people   most writing   artwork
privately owned websites   music videos
dangerous information(bomb building, dangerous lies, etc.)

- Interview a classmate using the questions below.

  1. Are there things on the internet which you don't like? Describe them.
  2. Have you ever been blocked from going to a website?

Internet Censorship

🟠 **Read the passage.**

It is true that the internet can be a dangerous place. There are websites which teach bomb-making and provide information on terrorist activity. Other websites send viruses which can steal your personal information and destroy your computer. The internet is also full of violent and sexual content. Many people feel that this is very inappropriate, especially for children.

Censoring the internet is one possible solution. It is a way of controlling information, specifically harmful information. Many believe that it is impossible to completely censor the internet. Governments cannot regulate laws of other countries. Internet users can find banned information from other countries with less strict regulations. And some people oppose censorship because they feel that it interferes with freedom of speech and expression.

China has some of the strictest internet censorship laws in the world. They also monitor what people say on the internet. They claim it is to protect citizens and create a united country. Critics worry that the government is using censorship to control its citizens. Many people have been arrested for signing online petitions, saying bad things about the government, or for talking to people in other countries. People are not free to say what they believe.

Governments claim that they use censorship to protect citizens against dangerous and offensive material. Other people see it as a way of controlling people. What do you think?

Comprehension Check   Answer the questions.

1. How is the internet a dangerous place?
2. Why might it be impossible to censor the internet?
3. Why do some people oppose internet censorship?
4. Which country has the strictest internet censorship laws?
5. Why have so many people been arrested in China?

Vocabulary Check   Complete the sentence with a word from the box.

offensive	specifically	petition	monitor	banned

1. I don't like sports, _____ violent sports like boxing.
2. Please don't speak when I am talking. I find it _____.
3. The council _____ talking on cell phones while driving.
4. Would you like to sign the _____ to save the whales?
5. Your tutor will _____ your progress in school to make sure you are not falling behind.

Think About It

Think about the advantages and disadvantages of internet censorship.

Advantages
- Protect children from inappropriate content
-
-

Disadvantages
- The government will monitor everything you do on the internet.
-
-

Opinion Practice

● **Practice supporting/refuting the opinions.**

Supporting Opinions

1. Parents should monitor what their children do on the computer... _____
2. Violent and sexual content should be banned from the internet... _____
3. It is impossible to completely censor the internet... _____
4. We should not arrest people for saying what they believe... _____

> a. since governments cannot regulate what people in other countries do.
> b. because people should be allowed to express their opinions and have free speech.
> c. because many websites are inappropriate for children.
> d. because it is offensive material.

Refuting Opinions

1. Governments only use internet censorship to control what people think. _____
2. Every country should make the same laws about internet censorship. It will be easier to regulate that way. _____
3. The internet should be banned because it is too dangerous. _____
4. Internet censorship protects us from offensive content. _____

> a. That's a bad idea. Countries should make laws based on what the people want. Every country does not want the same thing.
> b. I disagree. I think they use censorship to protect us from harmful information.
> c. That's not necessarily true. It can also be used to control what we read, think, and say.
> d. No it isn't. The internet is a very useful tool and is pretty safe. There are only some small problems which need fixing.

Opinion Examples

○ Read the opinions and answer the questions.

Track 14

❝ I think that internet censorship is a good thing. The internet is a scary place. There are many violent videos and they are easy to find. I always see inappropriate advertisements when I am trying to do research for school. They are very offensive to me and I don't want to see them. Once I even downloaded a virus to my computer because I opened spam mail. Internet censorship would keep me safe. I would be happy if this information was banned. ❞

Opinion B

Track 15

❝ I think that internet censorship is bad for people and for society. Internet censorship prevents us from finding all the information we want. And we cannot say what we believe or we will be punished. It is a way to control what we read and say. Governments can even block information which hurts politicians or very rich companies. They can also monitor what people say and do on the internet. If someone says that they are not happy with the government they can be arrested. We are not free with internet censorship, and that makes me afraid. ❞

1. Please circle the main idea in each opinion.
2. Please underline the supporting ideas in each opinion.
3. What could you say to further support the opinion with which you agree?

Discussion Questions

● **Discuss the questions in groups.**

1. Do you think people should use their real name when using the internet? Why or why not?

2. Families should decide how to censor the internet, not the government. Do you agree?

3. Is it right for the government to monitor what people say and do on the internet?

4. Many people think that China's internet censorship laws are too strict. Do you think they are OK, or should they be changed?

5. People often want what they cannot have. Would people be more likely to look at censored websites just because they are censored?

Expression Tips

Refuting Expressions

I don't understand why ~

I object ~

I see things differently.

Choose one statement. Debate the statement in groups.
(One group agrees with the statement, the other group disagree with the statement.)

1. Internet censorship is unnecessary. There is a lot of offensive material on the internet, but you don't have to look at it.

2. Everyone should have free access to information. We have a right to know and see whatever we want.

3. In the future it will be possible to completely censor the internet.

UNIT 6 CCTV

Warm-up

- Fill in the diagram with pros and cons of having a CCTV in your classroom.

Pros	Cons
protect students	less privacy

- Interview a classmate using the questions below.

1. Have you ever seen a CCTV camera? Where have you seen them?
2. Would you feel safe if CCTVs were in your school? Explain why or why not.

CCTV

Read the passage.

Closed-circuit television, or CCTV, uses video cameras to transmit a video signal to a specific location. The signal is not openly transmitted and only certain people can view it. It is often used in places where security is very important, like banks, airports, and schools.

Many believe CCTVs deter crime. They think people are less likely to commit a crime if they know they are being watched. Similarly, CCTVs can detect dangerous activity when it is occurring. The footage provides evidence for lawyers and police officers. This gives people a sense of security. News stations use CCTV systems to monitor traffic and report any delays to drivers. They are also used in places which are not safe for humans. This allows people to monitor a situation without risking lives.

Innocent people, however, do not like to be watched all the time. This creates mutual distrust between people and the government and fears about invasion of privacy. There is also little evidence to suggest that they deter crime. A 2008 report by United Kingdom Police Chiefs estimated that only 3% of crimes were deterred because of CCTVs. It is possible that people will simply go to places without cameras to commit crimes. Installing a CCTV system comes at great expense as people must buy, install, and monitor the cameras.

The debate about whether or not CCTVs are effective will go on. Should we continue to make them better, or find alternative ways of ensuring security?

Comprehension Check Answer the questions.

1. How do CCTVs work?
2. How can CCTVs help deter crime?
3. Why are CCTVs expensive?
4. How do CCTVs help drivers?
5. In 2008, what percent of crimes were deterred in the UK because of CCTVs?

Vocabulary Check Complete the sentence with a word from the box.

evidence	alternative	transmit	detect	mutual

1. Do you _____ that smell? I think it is chocolate!
2. I don't like this restaurant. Do you have a(n) _____?
3. Before making his decision, the judge looked at all of the _____.
4. Scientists can _____ signals to satellites in space.
5. The enemies may not like each other, but they have _____ respect for each other.

Think About It

Think about the advantages and disadvantages of CCTV.

Advantages
- Provides evidence for lawyers and police officers
-
-

Disadvantages
- Can create mutual distrust between people and the government
-
-

Opinion Practice

● **Practice supporting/refuting the opinions.**

Supporting Opinions

1. Schools should have CCTV cameras... _____
2. CCTVs should be used in places which are dangerous for people... _____
3. People should have a right to privacy... _____
4. The police should use video cameras when solving crimes... _____

> a. because it is uncomfortable to be watched all the time.
> b. because it provides great evidence for finding criminals.
> c. since they allow people to monitor a place without risking human lives.
> d. because they help protect students and teachers.

Refuting Opinions

1. Cameras are better than police officers for stopping crimes from happening. _____
2. CCTVs should be banned because they invade our privacy. _____
3. If you put a CCTV camera in your home it will stop people from robbing your house. _____
4. People feel safe because of CCTVs. _____

> a. Not all people feel that way. Some feel uncomfortable being watched all of the time.
> b. That's not necessarily true. Someone may still rob your house, but you will have evidence to catch them.
> c. I disagree. Criminals are more afraid of the police than cameras.
> d. That's not true. They protect our privacy by preventing criminals from hurting and robbing us.

Opinion Examples

● **Read the opinions and answer the questions.**

Opinion A

Track 17

❝ I feel safe at school because of CCTVs. There are cameras in all of the hallways and classrooms. If something bad happens the school will know about it. One day something bad did happen. A man broke into the school. He damaged doors and windows and stole some computers. The police were able to find the man and arrest him because of the footage on the CCTVs. We got our computers back and have not had a robbery at the school since then. I think CCTVs should be in all schools. ❞

Opinion B

Track 18

❝ My school has CCTV cameras. I don't like it. I am a good person and I never cause any problems. I do not want to be watched all of the time when I am not doing anything wrong. I feel like the school administrators do not trust the students. I feel uncomfortable when I see the cameras. They are invading my privacy, and preventing me from acting normally while I am at school. I think they should be banned from all schools. ❞

1. Please circle the main idea in each opinion.
2. Please underline the supporting ideas in each opinion.
3. What could you say to further support the opinion with which you agree?

Discussion Questions

● **Discuss the questions in groups.**

1. Do you think that CCTV prevents crime?

2. Should people have the right to privacy in public places?

3. Hackers and criminals can also use CCTV to spy on people and gain information. How can we prevent this from happening?

4. Should schools ask students for permission to use CCTVs before they install them?

5. Should families put CCTVs in their homes for added security?

Expression Tips
<u>Refuting Expressions</u>
I'm opposed to ~
It doesn't make sense.
That's why I can't agree with you on your point.

Time to Debate

Choose one statement. Debate the statement in groups.
(One group agrees with the statement, the other group disagree with the statement.)

1. Police officers are more effective at preventing crime than CCTV cameras. We should hire more police officers instead of installing more cameras.

2. CCTVs are expensive. It would be better to spend this money on teacher salaries and financial aid for students.

3. People feel safe when they are in a place with CCTVs.

UNIT 7 Privacy of Public Figures

Warm-up

● **Match the public figures in List A with the reason they are a public figure in List B.**

List A	List B
1. President of a country	a. They are often seen in films.
2. Mayor of a city	b. They are often seen playing sports
3. Famous actor	c. Is the leader of a country.
4. Famous musician	d. Entertains many people with songs.
5. Famous athlete	e. Makes decisions for a city.
6. Leader of an animal rights group	f. Informs people about the rights of animals.

- Besides the people in List A, who else can be a public figure?
- Name three places where you feel that you have the most privacy.

● **Interview a classmate using the questions below.**

1. Who is your favorite celebrity? Why do you like that person?
2. Have you ever met a public figure? Who would you like to meet?

Privacy of Public Figures

🟠 Read the passage.

Track 19

A fairly high level of public activity is needed to become a public figure. They can be politicians or other elected officials, celebrities, athletes, or community leaders. We regularly see their names and pictures in the news, magazines and on TV. Many people believe that public figures have fewer rights to privacy than others. Should they be granted the same level of privacy as everyone else?

Many believe they should not. Public figures are in a position of power. Their opinions affect our lives and influence our decisions. Politicians and community leaders make laws, while celebrities and athletes act as role models. Their salaries are even paid for by the taxes people pay and the money spent on entertainment. People have a right to know if they are behaving appropriately and honestly. It would be unfair if they abused their power at our personal and financial expense.

Others believe it is not fair to judge public figures at such a high standard. It puts increased pressure and stress on their lives, and the lives of their families and friends. Everyone should be treated equally regardless of their occupation. Public figures are often harassed and photographed by the media. Reporters and paparazzi have even broken the law to get pictures of celebrities. In 1997, a tragic event occurred when Princess Diana and two other people were killed in a car accident. They were fleeing the paparazzi.

Comprehension Check Answer the questions.

1. What is needed to become a public figure?
2. Give four examples of people who can be a public figure.
3. Who pays for the salaries of public figures?
4. Who sometimes breaks the law to get pictures of celebrities?
5. In what year did Princess Diana die?

Vocabulary Check Complete the sentence with a word from the box.

| taxes | harass | appropriately | officials | granted |

1. You should not _____ members of the opposing team. It is bad sportsmanship.
2. I feel like 40% is too much money to pay on _____.
3. You are not dressed _____ for school. You will have to go home and change.
4. I was _____ a visa to work in the USA for one year.
5. The _____ at work decided that there will be an office party once a month.

Think About It

Answer the questions below.

1. Would you like to be a public figure? Explain why or why not.

2. Would you like to work as a paparazzi? Explain why or why not.

3. How are reporters good for our society?

Opinion Practice

● **Practice supporting/refuting the opinions.**

Supporting Opinions

1. We should respect our public figures... _____
2. Public figures should respect the public... _____
3. The paparazzi should be arrested... _____
4. Politicians are more important than movie stars... _____

> a. because we pay their salaries.
>
> b. since they make laws while actors only entertain us.
>
> c. because they are too aggressive and invade the privacy of public figures.
>
> d. because they are successful people who make important decisions and influence our lives.

Refuting Opinions

1. Only celebrities and politicians can become public figures. _____
2. If you become a public figure you must also become a perfect citizen. _____
3. Everyone should have the right to privacy. _____
4. The paparazzi always break the laws and harass public figures. They should be arrested. _____

> a. That's impossible. Many people can be successful while still making mistakes. No one is perfect.
>
> b. That's not true. Anyone can become a public figure if they are involved in the community.
>
> c. That's not necessarily true. They are working hard just like anyone else. Most of them take their job seriously and respect the law.
>
> d. I disagree. I think it is important to know about the private lives of people who have power over your life.

Opinion Examples

● **Read the opinions and answer the questions.**

Opinion A

Track 20

❝ I feel bad for celebrities who are harassed by the paparazzi. The paparazzi make the lives of celebrities very stressful. Celebrities cannot walk down the street or go to a store without someone taking their picture. The paparazzi are sometimes very aggressive. They will even follow a celebrity for miles just to get a picture. Some paparazzi even break the law. They have even broken into celebrities' houses. They are the same as stalkers. It must be very frustrating to be a celebrity. It should be illegal to be a paparazzi. ❞

Opinion B

Track 21

❝ I love looking at pictures of my favorite celebrities in magazines. I enjoy seeing where they live and what stores they shop in. Celebrities are so cool, and I want to be just like them. They are role models to many people. They should accept the fact that other people care so much about their lives. Celebrities become more popular because of these pictures, too. It is great for their career, and fun for the fans. Celebrities should be happy that the paparazzi are taking their picture. ❞

1. Please circle the main idea in each opinion.
2. Please underline the supporting ideas in each opinion.
3. What would you say to further support the opinion with which you agree?

Discussion Questions

● **Discuss the questions in groups.**

1. Is it healthy that people have so much interest in the lives of public figures?

2. Is it fair that public figures are judged at a higher standard than the rest of us?

3. Who is to blame for the increased interest in the lives of celebrities and politicians? The media or the public?

4. How would your life change if you became a public figure?

5. Many people think that being photographed is part of the job of a public figure. Their lack of privacy is the price they pay for being rich and powerful. Do you agree? Why or why not?

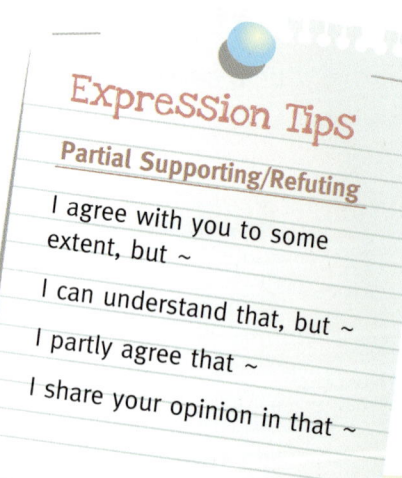

Expression Tips

Partial Supporting/Refuting

I agree with you to some extent, but ~

I can understand that, but ~

I partly agree that ~

I share your opinion in that ~

Choose one statement. Debate the statement in groups.
(One group agrees with the statement, the other group disagree with the statement.)

1. Everyone should be treated equally regardless of their occupation.

2. People exaggerate the problem concerning the privacy of public figures. They actually have a very private life.

3. A person's right to know is more important than a person's privacy.

UNIT 8 Fashion

Warm-up

- **What kind of fashion do these people usually wear? Match the styles with the people.**

People	Their fashion style
Pop singers	trendy new outfits, lots of jewelry
Golfers	
Businessmen	
Rappers	
Sports fans	
Your best friend	

- **Interview a classmate using the questions below.**

   1. What do you like to wear when you go to a party? Why do you like it?
   2. What kinds of clothes do your parents wear when they go to work?

47

Fashion

🟠 **Read the passage.**

Track 22

Fashion is everywhere. Magazines, television, and movies are full of beautiful people wearing the coolest outfits. People are exposed to fashion every day at home, school, work and in public places. But how does fashion affect our lives?

Fashion allows people to express their personality and interests. This will help you fit in with different social groups and make new friends. Employers are impressed by people who dress professionally. Fashion can make you more confident in yourself. It feels good to look nice and be complimented on your appearance. Someone might even ask you on a date because of your fashion style and added confidence.

Fashion has great potential, but serious problems, too. The fashion industry has often been blamed for society's problems with weight and eating disorders. Companies hire beautiful, skinny women and muscular men to model their clothes. Many people think they must look that way, too. Some fashion industries do not make clothes for overweight people, further stressing the importance of image and beauty. The most popular clothes are often expensive, which is a big strain on your finances. Some fashion companies exploit workers. They are given low wages and work long hours. They work hard to make us beautiful.

Fashion can be fun and enjoyable. It can also be an unhealthy and expensive burden. It is important to be aware of how fashion affects you and your life.

Comprehension Check — Answer the questions.

1. What does fashion allow people to do?
2. How can fashion help you impress employers?
3. Why has the fashion industry been blamed for society's problems with weight and eating disorders?
4. How do some fashion companies exploit workers?
5. Where are people exposed to fashion?

Vocabulary Check — Complete the sentence with a word from the box.

compliment	exploit	exposed	fit in with	outfits

1. It is wrong to _____ people who are less fortunate than you.
2. I would like to _____ you on your new haircut.
3. The workers were _____ to dangerous chemicals at the factory.
4. Mary has a great sense of fashion and always wears the newest _____.
5. I _____ the music club because I enjoy playing the guitar.

Think About It

Think about the advantages and disadvantages of fashion.

Advantages
- People can express their personality and interests.
-
-

Disadvantages
- Some companies exploit workers.
-
-

49

Opinion Practice

- **Practice supporting/refuting the opinions.**

Supporting Opinions

1. Schools should make students wear uniforms... _____
2. People who work in a business should wear suits... _____
3. Fashion companies should make their clothes for all sizes... _____
4. You should wear clothes that express your personality and interests... _____

> a. since you can impress employers and customers by dressing professionally.
>
> b. because fashion is a big distraction for students. Uniforms will make everyone the same.
>
> c. because it will help you to make friends and fit in with different social groups.
>
> d. because overweight people like to wear nice outfits and have good fashion, too.

Refuting Opinions

1. Fashion models should be role models because they look beautiful. _____
2. You should try to impress your friends by buying cool clothes. _____
3. Fashion companies should use cheap workers to save money. _____
4. Eating disorders are caused by fashion. _____

> a. No, you should wear clothes that you feel comfortable in.
>
> b. It is nice to be beautiful, but we should model our lives after people who stress inner beauty instead.
>
> c. That's a bad idea. It is wrong to exploit other people.
>
> d. That's not necessarily true. People get eating disorders for many different reasons.

Opinion Examples

● **Read the opinions and answer the questions.**

Opinion A

Track 23

❝ I think it is important to follow the latest fashions. Fashion helps people make friends and be accepted by different social groups. All of my friends at school wear nice outfits and jewelry. They look cool, and everyone likes them. People who wear ugly clothes or have bad fashion are teased and made fun of. If you don't wear nice outfits it will be hard to be popular. It is easy to know what fashions are popular, and wearing them can make your life more enjoyable. ❞

Opinion B

Track 24

❝ I don't think that fashion is very important. My friends spend too much time and money trying to look cool. They think that clothes make you popular. They are trying to impress other people and are not being themselves. Personality is more important than fashion. If you are a good person you will make friends. Some of the most popular people I know have very bad fashion, but people like them because they are nice and funny. You don't need to buy the latest clothes to be popular. ❞

1. Please circle the main idea in each opinion.
2. Please underline the supporting ideas in each opinion.
3. What would you say to further support the opinion with which you agree?

Discussion Questions

● **Discuss the questions in groups.**

1. Is it healthy for young people to diet to look like fashion models?

2. Kids today sometimes dress in very sexy outfits. Should children dress more conservatively?

3. Do you think that fashion advertisements should be banned from the media?

4. Should fashion companies be forced to make their outfits in all sizes? Is it OK for them to make clothes only for skinny people?

5. Should you use fashion to impress your friends?

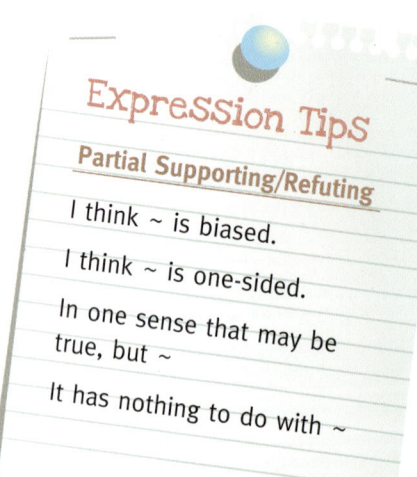

Expression Tips

Partial Supporting/Refuting

I think ~ is biased.

I think ~ is one-sided.

In one sense that may be true, but ~

It has nothing to do with ~

Choose one statement. Debate the statement in groups.
(One group agrees with the statement, the other group disagree with the statement.)

1. The fashion industry sometimes uses cheap workers from poor parts of the world. Many people consider exploiting workers to be wrong. It should be stopped.

2. Uniforms make everyone look the same. It would be better if people wore uniforms at school and at work.

3. Inner beauty is more important than your appearance.

UNIT 9 Advertisement

Warm-up

- Describe the following advertisement. Use at least 3 adjectives for it.

Best cell phone in the world

Our company's new cell phone is the best cell phone in the world. It is stylish and cool, and everyone will be jealous that you own one. You can make calls, text friends, use the internet, and it is also a flashlight!!! You can use it anywhere without losing a call. It is small, and the battery life lasts for 5 days. Buy one today for only $500.

Buy one today for only $500

- How would you describe it?
- Would you buy this product? Yes / No

- Interview a classmate using the questions below.

1. Do you have a favorite commercial on TV or on the internet? Describe it.
2. What was the last advertisement you saw? Where did you see it?

Advertisement

🟠 **Read the passage.**

Track 25

Advertising is the best way to inform customers about products and services. It increases public awareness of goods and recognition for companies. Many jobs are created because of advertising. People are required to make, transport and sell advertised goods. This benefits the entire economy. As more goods are produced and sold, companies become richer and can afford to sell their products at a lower price. This creates competition between companies and allows the consumer to save money. Ads can be used to educate and motivate the public, too. They inform people about important issues like AIDS, deforestation, and world hunger.

Advertisements, however, are not always beneficial. They play on our emotions and try to make us want things we don't need. Sometimes advertisers give misleading information to make us believe a product is the best. Young children are especially vulnerable, and many ads are aimed directly at kids. Advertisers use this to turn children into life-long customers and influence the decisions of their parents. Advertising also sends the message that image and beauty are important. Sexy women and muscular men are used to sell everything from clothes to cars and soap.

We are exposed to advertisements everyday in newspapers, television, the internet, billboards and less obvious places. While advertising is great for the economy, it can have negative effects on the family. We must be careful not to let advertisements trick us into buying inferior products and things we don't need.

Comprehension Check Answer the questions.

1. How do advertisements create jobs?
2. How can ads educate and motivate the public?
3. Why do advertisers give misleading information?
4. Why do some advertisers aim their ads at children?
5. Where can we find advertisements?

Vocabulary Check Complete the sentence with a word from the box.

| misleading | billboard | consumers | goods | obvious |

1. The _____ were made in India and sold in the USA.
2. I saw an advertisement for your restaurant on a(n) _____ outside.
3. The test was easy. Most of the answers were _____.
4. I was confused because the information was very _____.
5. The store had a big sale today. The _____ were given 50% off all items.

Think About It

Think about the advantages and disadvantages of advertisement.

Advantages
- It's the best way to inform people about new products and services.
-
-

Disadvantages
- Some advertisements try to make us want things we don't need.
-
-

Opinion Practice

● **Practice supporting/refuting the opinions.**

Supporting Opinions

1. You should pay attention to the ads you see... _____
2. Children under 5 years old should not watch TV... _____
3. Ads should not be allowed to give misleading information... _____
4. Advertising is great for the economy... _____

> a. because they are too vulnerable to the commercials and advertisements.
> b. because it is important to be honest with customers.
> c. because it creates jobs and spreads money to different people.
> d. since they may be about a new product you need.

Refuting Opinions

1. You should ignore advertisements because there is too much misleading information. _____
2. Companies should not spend so much money on advertising. _____
3. People should not waste their money on things they don't need. _____
4. Advertising should be allowed in schools. _____

> a. I don't agree. Everyone should be allowed to buy anything that makes them happy, as long as they can afford it.
> b. That's not true. Most ads give accurate information.
> c. No, it shouldn't. Students need to focus on learning and not be distracted by ads at school.
> d. I disagree. It is important for companies to inform customers about new products. That's how they make more money.

Opinion Examples

● Read the opinions and answer the questions.

Track 26

❝ Companies should stop stressing the importance of image and appearance to sell their products. Advertisers make their products look cool and try to convince us that we will be cool if we buy them. Companies use popular images and even hire celebrities to be in their ads. Beautiful people are used to sell the simplest products like pencils and books. This sends the wrong image to the public that being cool is important. Instead, companies should focus on how the product will help us and why it is good, not why it will make us cool. ❞

Opinion B

Track 27

❝ I think that image and appearance is an important part of advertising. Everyone has different interests and personalities. Ads can present a certain image to try and sell their products to specific groups of people. I don't like things which are violent, so I would not buy a violent video game; however, I do like things which are fun and romantic. If a new movie ad presented the image of a cute, lovable character, I would probably watch it. Its image and appearance would match the things which I enjoy. ❞

1. Please circle the main idea in each opinion.

2. Please underline the supporting ideas in each opinion.

3. What could you say to further the opinion with which you agree?

Discussion Questions

● **Discuss the questions in groups.**

1. Do you think advertising should be allowed in schools?

2. Does advertising also help regulate the quality of goods?

3. If it were allowed, what kind of advertisements do you think should be banned?

4. How would the world be different if advertising was banned from all media?

5. Can we blame advertising for making people unhealthy and making bad lifestyle choices?

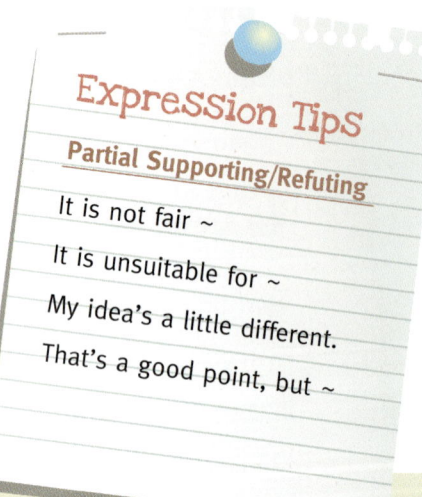

Expression Tips
Partial Supporting/Refuting
It is not fair ~
It is unsuitable for ~
My idea's a little different.
That's a good point, but ~

Time to Debate

Choose one statement. Debate the statement in groups.
(One group agrees with the statement, the other group disagree with the statement.)

1. Children under 5 years old are too young to see advertisements.

2. The image of a product is more important than how it helps us.

3. People are more likely to buy a product that is advertised than a product which is not well advertised.

UNIT 10 Legacy Preference

Warm-up

- Besides good grades, what other qualities, skills and achievements can help a student to get accepted to a university? Fill in the table.

Qualities	Skills	Achievements
leadership	good at sports	winning academic awards

- Interview a classmate using the questions below.

  1. Did your parents go to college? Where did they go?
  2. Do you have any older brothers and sisters? Are they thinking about going to college? What about your friends? Are they thinking about college already?

Legacy Preference

Read the passage.

Many universities give special preference to applicants known as legacies. Legacies have a family member, normally a parent, who graduated from that university. These alumni usually donate significant amounts of money to the school. In exchange, their children have a better chance of being admitted.

Admitting legacies helps to maintain a strong alumni relationship and can benefit every student. Private universities rely heavily on alumni donations. These donations support improvements for the school, and fund financial aid. This lessens the burden of poor families to pay for an education they otherwise could not afford. It can increase equality in education as a more diverse group of students can attend the university. The alumni may even help graduates find jobs. Strong alumni relationships also build a sense of tradition and school pride.

Opponents find this policy to be unfair. They think it gives an undeserved advantage to the students who need the least help. Legacies usually come from well-educated families that are financially secure. Poor students who are just as qualified may not get accepted and become upset. They will believe that success is based on money and not academic merits. Some legacies even feel uncomfortable being labeled a legacy. They fear the only reason they were admitted was because of their parents' money, not their abilities.

Comprehension Check — Answer the questions.

1. What is a legacy?
2. What do alumni get in exchange for donating time and money to a school?
3. How do universities use donated money?
4. Where do legacies usually come from?
5. Why do some legacies feel uncomfortable being labeled a legacy?

Vocabulary Check — Complete the sentence with a word from the box.

alumni	prefer	policy	applicants	donate

1. My friends like to _____ their old clothes to the homeless.
2. My school has a(n) _____ of giving financial aid to all students who need it.
3. The admissions officer had a difficult job because the _____ were all very qualified.
4. I don't like those shoes. I _____ the blue ones.
5. There is a(n) _____ dinner every year at graduation.

Think About It

Think about the advantages and disadvantages of legacy preference.

Advantages
- It lessens the burden on poor families to pay for school.
-
-

Disadvantages
- Gives an undeserved advantage to people who need the least help.
-
-

Opinion Practice

- **Practice supporting/refuting the opinions.**

Supporting Opinions

1. Every school should give financial aid... _____
2. Universities should ban legacy preference... _____
3. Alumni should donate money to the university they graduated from... _____
4. Academics, not money, should be the most important part of a university... _____

> a. because we go to a university to learn.
>
> b. because it gives an unfair advantage to students who don't need help.
>
> c. since it helps poor students pay for school and increases equality in education.
>
> d. because their children will have a better chance of being accepted when they apply.

Refuting Opinions

1. Only rich people can get into the best colleges. _____
2. Private universities should ban legacy preference. _____
3. Donating money to a university will guarantee that your child gets accepted. _____
4. If you are a legacy other students will be jealous of you and not like you. _____

> a. That's not necessarily true. Many legacies don't get accepted. They still must have good grades.
>
> b. No, they shouldn't. Private schools should have the right to admit anyone they want.
>
> c. That's not true. Financial aid helps all people in need attend college.
>
> d. I don't agree. You will be treated the same as everyone else as long as you are a good person and respectful.

Opinion Examples

Read the opinions and answer the questions.

Track 29

❝ The legacy preference policy should be banned at all schools. It gives an unfair advantage to students who don't need help. Schools should be helping people who actually need help, like poor and disadvantaged students. I come from a poor family, but I work hard at school. I should have the same chance to get into the best colleges as everyone else. I may not get accepted because a legacy takes my spot. It is not fair to people like me. ❞

Opinion B

Track 30

❝ Schools should be allowed to use legacy preference if they want to. It is great for keeping school tradition and building a strong alumni relationship. I go to a university which uses legacy preference. I always see alumni walking around campus and talking to current students. They share stories and experiences. They also share their money, and I received financial aid because of alumni donations. I even got a job working with an alumni from my school. Legacy preference helps everyone, not just legacies. ❞

1. Please circle the main idea in each opinion.
2. Please underline the supporting ideas in each opinion.
3. What would you say to further explain the opinion with which you agree?

Discussion Questions

● **Discuss the questions in groups.**

1. Being a legacy can help you get into some universities. How much should these universities consider a person's legacy status in the application process?

2. If legacy preference was banned, would it still be OK for schools to give preference to students who are excellent athletes?

3. If you were given an advantage getting into school, would you accept it?

4. How would you feel if you were a legacy? Would you be excited or uncomfortable about it?

5. How important are extracurricular activities, like being in a club or playing sports, when applying to college? Are they as important as getting good grades or being a legacy?

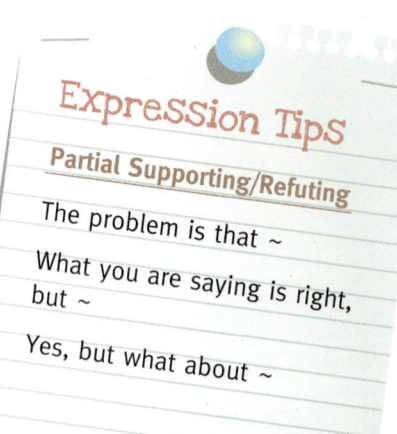

Expression Tips
Partial Supporting/Refuting
The problem is that ~
What you are saying is right, but ~
Yes, but what about ~

Choose one statement. Debate the statement in groups.
(One group agrees with the statement, the other group disagree with the statement.)

1. Legacy preference teaches students that fair competition is not important.

2. Diversity in education is more important than simply admitting the smartest, richest students.

3. Universities are too expensive. It is not fair to poor families who cannot afford to go. School should be free for everyone.

UNIT 11 Cloning

Warm-up

- **Cloning technology would make it possible to design a person with all of the best qualities. If you could design a clone, what characteristics, qualities and appearance would you give it?**

Appearance	Characteristics & Qualities
tall, blonde hair	kind, smart

- **Interview a classmate using the questions below.**

    1. Would you like to have a clone of yourself? Why or why not?
    2. If you could clone one person, who would it be? Why?

Cloning

🟠 **Read the passage.**

Cloning used to be just an idea in science fiction movies and books, but not anymore. Dolly the sheep was born on July 5, 1996. She was the first mammal to successfully be cloned. Her birth introduced cloning to the world.

Scientists can learn much about genetics by studying cloning. They could fight genetic diseases like hemophilia. And they could make babies with desirable traits such as being tall. If organs could be cloned it would save the lives of people who need transplants. It could also be a solution to infertility and help families have children. We could produce disease resistant plants and animals with increased nutrition to fight world hunger. Or we could reproduce species which are endangered and close to extinction.

On the other hand, cloning may hamper the diversity of genes. Cloning, by definition, is making an exact copy of cells. Genetic diversity is important to help us adapt to changes and resist diseases. Diversity can also be beautiful. Having everything the same would be boring. There are ethical and moral issues to consider, and some see cloning as humans "playing God." Many believe it devalues human life as babies could be created in a laboratory. It is also possible that babies would deliberately be born with undesirable traits like aggressiveness.

There is still much to be learned about cloning. As it becomes more of an everyday reality, we must consider the positive and negative effects it will have on our lives.

Comprehension Check — Answer the questions.

1. When was Dolly the sheep born?
2. Why was Dolly's birth so important?
3. How could cloning help fight world hunger?
4. What is so important about genetic diversity?
5. How would cloning devalue human life?

Vocabulary Check — Complete the sentence with a word from the box.

| deliberately | genes | infertility | hampered | endangered |

1. The couple had to adopt a child because of the husband's _____.
2. Blue whales are a(n) _____ species. There are only about 2,500 of them left in the ocean.
3. It is possible for scientists to cure diseases by studying our _____.
4. You _____ tried to make me fall!
5. My ability to play soccer is _____ by my sprained ankle.

Think About It

Think about the advantages and disadvantages of cloning.

Advantages
- Allow infertile couples to have a baby
-
-

Disadvantages
- It's a way for people to "play God."
-
-

67

Opinion Practice

- **Practice supporting/refuting the opinions.**

Supporting Opinions

1. Cloning should be banned... _____
2. Doctors should investigate the medical possibilities of cloning... _____
3. Farmers should consider cloning their best plants... _____
4. We should clone endangered species... _____

   a. because then all of their produce would be of the highest quality.
   b. since it would prevent them from becoming extinct.
   c. because it devalues human life and can potentially be misused.
   d. because it could help save the lives of many people.

Refuting Opinions

1. Scientists who study cloning are trying to be like "God." _____
2. Cloning should be left in the science fiction movies. It is too dangerous for real life. _____
3. Everyone should have a clone to use for spare body parts if they are sick. _____
4. Cloning should be banned. _____

   a. That's a terrible reason to have a clone. A clone is alive, and we should respect its rights. We should clone organs instead.
   b. That's not necessarily true. As we learn more about cloning it may become a completely safe procedure.
   c. That's foolish to say. They are only trying to understand the human body and help people.
   d. I disagree. I think we should continue to research cloning because it might positively affect our lives.

Opinion Examples

● Read the opinions and answer the questions.

Track 32

❝ I think cloning would benefit society. The medical possibilities are many. Cloning can help scientists find cures for diseases. We can learn more about how the human body works. We would also make our plants and animals stronger and healthier. We could clone the best plants and animals and fight world hunger. I could even clone my favorite pet so that I could have it with me all my life! We need to investigate the possibilities of cloning further, as it could help all people, animals and plants. ❞

Opinion B

Track 33

❝ I think cloning should be banned. Cloning could be used for good, but it could also be used for evil. The military could clone super-soldiers to be used for war. And we don't know enough about genetic diversity to safely say that cloning is safe. Mistakes could happen, and it's possible that we could kill an entire species of plants or animals by accident. I don't think that cloning is worth the risk to society, animals and plants. ❞

1. Please circle the main idea in each opinion.

2. Please underline the supporting ideas in each opinion.

3. What would you say to further support the opinion with which you agree?

Discussion Questions

● **Discuss the questions in groups.**

1. Can cloning be used for evil? How?

2. Would you eat food that has been cloned?

3. What would it be like to be a clone?

4. Does cloning a baby in a laboratory devalue human life?

5. Would you like to have a clone of your favorite pet if it died?

Expression Tips

Partial Supporting/Refuting

You are right, but ~
You're missing the point.
You've got a point there, but ~

Time to Debate

Choose one statement. Debate the statement in groups.
(One group agrees with the statement, the other group disagree with the statement.)

1. The benefits of cloning outweigh the risks.

2. A clone is still human. The clone should have all the same rights as us.

3. There are ethical issues with cloning humans, but there should be no problem cloning plants.

UNIT 12 Death Penalty

Warm-up

● Match the following crimes with what you think is the most appropriate punishment.

Death penalty	Go to jail	Pay a fine

steal a car　　　　　　　　rob a bank　　　　　　　get in a big fight
get a parking ticket　　　　murder　　　　　　　　driving too fast
littering　　　　　　　　　kidnapping　　　　　　　treason
sending computer viruses　　insurance fraud　　　　　terrorism
child abuse　　　　　　　　breaking a window

● Interview a classmate using the questions below.

1. Does your country allow the death penalty? Do you know of any countries that allow the death penalty?

2. Can criminals change and become good members of society?

Death Penalty

🔴 **Read the passage.**

Track 34

The death penalty is the premeditated killing by the government of a person convicted of certain crimes. Many countries allow the death penalty as a way to protect citizens from very dangerous people. Others believe it is the same as murder.

Proponents see the death penalty as a crime deterrent. People will be less likely to commit murder if they know the penalty for it is death. Ethically, some people believe that you give up your right to life if you kill another human. Families of victims would be given closure and be able to move on with their lives. It would also help the prison system. Prisons are very overpopulated with not enough space to hold everyone. This would free space, and protect guards and other inmates from a criminal attacking again in prison.

Opponents believe the death penalty sends the wrong message to society. It is hypocritical to execute someone to show that killing is wrong. It's also possible to kill an innocent person, which has happened in the past. Others see life in prison as a worse punishment and a better deterrent to crime. It may even create sympathy for criminals, making people forget the evil they have done. Studies also show that the death penalty costs more money than sentencing a person to life in prison. This is because of an endless appeal system and additional procedures which cost a lot of money.

Comprehension Check   Answer the questions.

1. What is the death penalty?
2. Why would people be less likely to commit a crime?
3. How does the death penalty help the prison system?
4. How does the death penalty help the families of victims?
5. Why is the death penalty more expensive than keeping a person in prison for life?

Vocabulary Check   Complete the sentence with a word from the box.

| executed | sentence | inmates | closure | sympathy |

1. Less than 100 people are _____ annually in the United States of America.
2. The convict received a 5 year _____ for stealing a car.
3. There are too many _____ in the prison and not enough rooms.
4. I felt _____ for my friend when he lost his cell phone.
5. I just took my final exam. It brought _____ to the school year and introduced the beginning of summer vacation.

Think About It

Think about the advantages and disadvantages of the death penalty.

Advantages
- Protects citizens from very dangerous people
-
-

Disadvantages
- Giving a life sentence is a better crime deterrent and a worse punishment.
-
-

Opinion Practice

- **Practice supporting/refuting the opinions.**

Supporting Opinions

1. The death penalty is the best way to deter crime... _____
2. You should not feel sympathy for criminals... _____
3. We should ban the death penalty... _____
4. Sentencing some to life in prison is a better deterrent to crime than the death penalty... _____

> a. because it is hypocritical to kill someone to show that killing is wrong.
>
> b. because people will not commit a crime if the sentence for it is death.
>
> c. since they are a horrible place where you cannot be free and are in constant danger.
>
> d. because they are bad people who have done bad things.

Refuting Opinions

1. Some crimes are so terrible that the criminal should be put to death. _____
2. The death penalty is the best deterrent to crime. _____
3. Life in prison is a worse sentence than death. _____
4. Inmates do not deserve to be protected when they are in prison. _____

> a. I disagree. I think it is wrong to kill people for any reason.
>
> b. Everyone deserves to be safe, even convicts. Crimes are illegal in jail, too, and convicts should be safe from violence.
>
> c. No, it isn't. Dying is the worst punishment possible. There is no chance to become a better person and have a good life.
>
> d. That's not true. People still commit serious crimes even though the death penalty is legal.

Opinion Examples

- Read the opinions and answer the questions.

Track 35

❝ The death penalty should be banned. It is wrong to kill someone to show that killing is wrong. It is hypocritical of the government to do this, and it sets a bad example for society. Also, the death penalty is expensive. It takes a lot of time and money before the convict is executed, and it would be cheaper to give a life sentence. I even think that a life sentence is a better deterrent to crime because prisons are a horrible place. ❞

Opinion B

Track 36

❝ The death penalty should not be banned. Criminals deserve to be punished for their crimes. Some crimes are so bad, like murder, that it's not safe for that person to live in society anymore. The only solution is death. The death penalty also serves as a crime deterrent. I would not commit a crime which would give me the death penalty. And it helps to make more room in an already overcrowded prison system. I think that while the penalty is harsh, sometimes it is deserved and it can help the rest of society. ❞

1. Please circle the main idea in each opinion.

2. Please underline the supporting ideas in each opinion.

3. What would you say to further support the opinion with which you agree?

Discussion Questions

● **Discuss the questions in groups.**

1. Does the death penalty help the families of victims?

2. Some convicts are able to change their lives and become good people while in prison. Should prisoners with a death sentence still be executed if they are able to change their life?

3. How effective is the death penalty in deterring crime?

4. Is it wrong to kill someone to show that killing is wrong?

5. Is it wrong to sympathize with criminals who are sentenced to death?

Expression Tips

Emphasizing Expressions

As I have mentioned before ~
As we already know ~
As you know ~

Choose one statement. Debate the statement in groups.
(One group agrees with the statement, the other group disagree with the statement.)

1. You should give up your right to life if you kill another person.

2. Life in prison is a better crime deterrent than the death sentence.

3. Instead of executing dangerous people, we should try to help them to be better people.

UNIT 13 Abortion

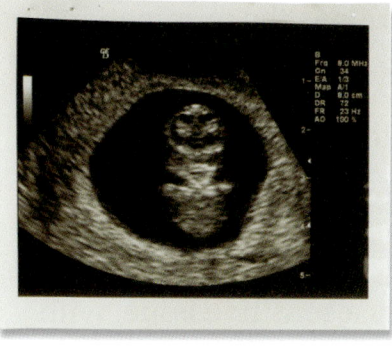
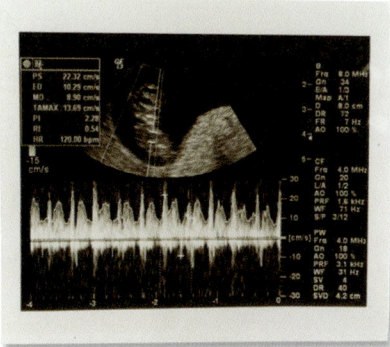
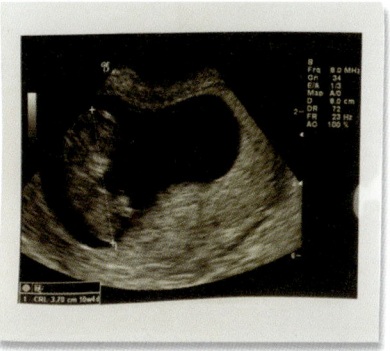

Warm-up

ED2-13
MP3

- Fill in the circles with reasons why someone might want to have an abortion.

- Interview a classmate using the questions below.

  1. Is it ever OK to hurt another person? When would it be OK?
  2. Why do you think that people have abortions?

Abortion

🟠 **Read the passage.**

An abortion is the termination of a pregnancy before a child is born. It is estimated that there are 42 million abortions worldwide every year. Many are done legally, others are not. It is a sensitive issue, with people supporting each side of the discussion.

Many argue that the government should not be allowed to tell a person what they can do with their body. Women should be allowed to choose to have their baby or not. Rape victims also argue for abortion. Having the child could be a constant reminder of the suffering they went through. If abortions were banned some women would still try and do it illegally. This would be very dangerous and laws would have to be created to combat it. It may also benefit all of society as unwanted children may be unloved and neglected.

Opponents argue that a fetus is human, and aborting it is the same as murder. Parents are denying a child the chance to life. Woman may also experience psychological problems like depression and guilt after the procedure. There are health risks involved like infection, recurring miscarriages, and sometimes death. Alternative choices also exist, like adoption. Many families want a child but can't have one. Adoption helps the mother, child and adopting family.

Is abortion wrong? Should women be allowed to decide the fate of their child? These are important questions to think about as we discuss the topic further.

Comprehension Check — Answer the questions.

1. How many abortions are believed to occur each year?
2. What would happen if abortions were banned?
3. What kind of psychological problems can women suffer from after having an abortion?
4. What are the health risks of having an abortion?
5. What is an alternative to abortion?

Vocabulary Check — Complete the sentence with a word from the box.

depression	combat	fetus	guilty	recurring

1. Every night Peter dreams that he is being chased by sharks. It is his _____ nightmare.
2. Police officers _____ crime every day.
3. Some people believe that a _____ is not a human until its mother gives birth.
4. Mary's _____ makes her feel very sad all of the time. We should help her to feel happy.
5. John felt _____ for taking his brother's sweater without asking.

Think About It

Think about the advantages and disadvantages of abortion.

Advantages
- It would help victims of rape forget about their suffering.
-
-

Disadvantages
- Women can experience psychological problems.
-
-

Opinion Practice

- **Practice supporting/refuting the opinions.**

Supporting Opinions

1. Abortion should be banned... _____
2. A mother should have the right to choose to have an abortion... _____
3. Fathers should help the mother decide if abortion is the right thing to do... _____
4. Banning abortion would be bad... _____

> a. because it is his child, too, and he should help decide the fate of his child.
> b. because it is her body and she can do what she wants with it.
> c. because women would still try and have illegal abortions, which are very dangerous.
> d. because you are denying a child a chance at life.

Refuting Opinions

1. Hospitals should not be allowed to perform abortions because hospitals are supposed to help people, not kill them. _____
2. A fetus is alive and should have the same rights as all humans. _____
3. Women would stop having abortions if they were illegal. _____
4. Women will feel guilty if they give their child up for adoption. _____

> a. Not always. I think they will feel happy knowing that they helped another couple start a family.
> b. I disagree. Sometimes having a baby can kill a mother. Doctor's would save her life by performing an abortion.
> c. No it's not. You are not human until you can live unsupported by another body.
> d. That's not necessarily true. Women may try to have illegal abortions, which are very dangerous.

Opinion Examples

- Read the opinions and answer the questions.

Opinion A

Track 38

❝ I believe that a woman should never have an abortion. Abortion is murder, and murder is wrong. No one should have the right to take the life of another person. The fetus is alive, and it deserves a chance at life. There is also an alternative which can help many people. If you don't want your child, you can put it up for adoption. That way another family can have a child and the child will be given an opportunity at life, too. ❞

Opinion B

Track 39

❝ I believe that in some situations abortions should be allowed. Sometimes women can die giving birth to a child. If having a baby would kill the mother, I think it would be OK to have an abortion. It would save the mother's life. I also think that abortions should be allowed in cases when a woman has been raped. Having the child might remind the woman of her suffering. Having an abortion would help her to get closure from a terrible event in her life. ❞

1. Please circle the main idea in each opinion.
2. Please underline the supporting ideas in each opinion.
3. What would you say to further support the argument with which you agree?

Discussion Questions

● **Discuss the questions in groups.**

1. Are there any situations where having an abortion would be OK?

2. What kinds of people are most likely to have an abortion?

3. Some people believe that a fetus is not human. At what point can we consider life to be human?

4. Adoption seems like a great alternative to abortion. What are some possible problems with adoption?

5. Why would a woman feel depression or guilt after having an abortion?

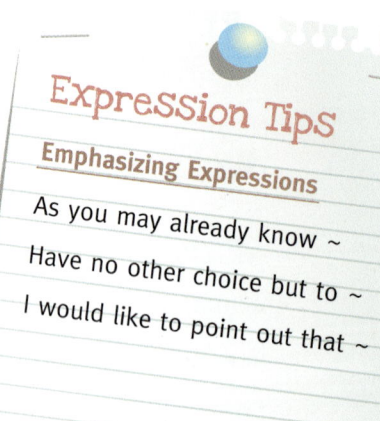

Expression Tips
Emphasizing Expressions
As you may already know ~
Have no other choice but to ~
I would like to point out that ~

Choose one statement. Debate the statement in groups.
(One group agrees with the statement, the other group disagree with the statement.)

1. The father of the child should be allowed to decide to have an abortion or not.

2. Everyone has the right to life. Under no circumstances should we be allowed to kill another person.

3. Abortion should be banned.

UNIT 14 Arranged Marriage

ED2-14
MP3

Warm-up

● Getting married is an important decision. What are some qualities that would be important in the person you marry?

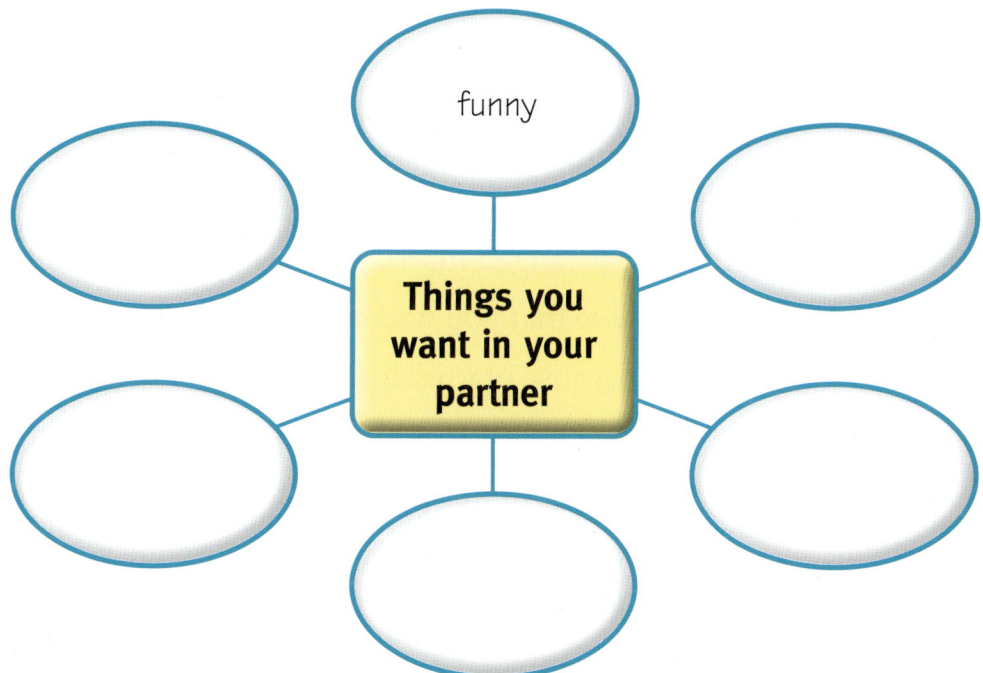

● Interview a classmate using the questions below.

1. Do your parents ever help you? Do they make decisions for you?
2. Would you let your parents choose your friends for you?

83

Arranged Marriage

● Read the passage.

Many people get married because they meet and fall in love. Some societies and religions, however, practice the tradition of arranged marriage. Almost always it involves the parents choosing who their child will marry.

The parents take great care to make sure their child's partner is a good match. They want the couple to be compatible ethnically, financially, religiously, and socially. There is usually a strong support system from both families in these relationships. The goal is for the couple to have the best future possible. Many couples find that love grows over time. For these reasons, the divorce rate of arranged marriages is far lower than that of other marriages. It also allows each person to focus on their career or studies while the parents choose a partner. Some groups, like the Orthodox Jews, even use it to make sure their culture and faith lasts into the future.

Many people frown upon this tradition. You can't experience the joys of dating and romantic love if you have an arranged marriage. You must obey and accept your parents' decision. It's possible that you won't like your chosen partner. But you must do what you are told because of pressure from your culture or religion.

It can be difficult to get out of a bad marriage because of this pressure, too. People who get married for love spend a long time getting to know each other first. This is often not possible in arranged marriages. Couples sometimes meet just before, or even at, the wedding.

Comprehension Check   Answer the questions.

1. Who often makes the decisions for an arranged marriage?
2. In which ways should an arranged couple be compatible?
3. Which type of marriage has a lower divorce rate, arranged or love marriages?
4. Why do the Orthodox Jews practice arranged marriage?
5. Why do some arranged couples not get to know each other before they are married?

Vocabulary Check   Complete the sentence with a word from the box.

a good match	tradition	partner	divorced	pressure

1. Every year we go to my grandmother's house on her birthday. It is a family _____.
2. There is too much _____ to get good grades in school.
3. That T-shirt looks cool. I think it is _____ for this hat.
4. Brian is getting married today. His marriage _____ is a woman named Sarah.
5. Steve's parents got _____ last year. They don't live together anymore.

Think About It

Think about the advantages and disadvantages of having an arranged marriage.

Advantages
- Lets you focus on your career or studies
-
-

Disadvantages
- Can't experience joys of dating and romantic love
-
-

Opinion Practice

- **Practice supporting/refuting the opinions.**

Supporting Opinions

1. You should be free to choose the person you want to marry... _____
2. You should do what your parents tell you to do... _____
3. Arranged marriages are bad... _____
4. People should be tolerant of the beliefs of other cultures and religions... _____

> a. because even if the things they do seem strange to us, they're important to them.
>
> b. because they raised you and know what is best for your future success.
>
> c. because a person is not free to choose the person they want to marry.
>
> d. because you will spend the rest of your life with that person and you will want to be happy.

Refuting Opinions

1. Arranged marriages should be banned in all cultures and religions. _____
2. Couples in an arranged marriage should stay together even if they are not compatible. _____
3. Love marriages are better than arranged marriages. _____
4. Your family should not influence your decision on who to marry. _____

> a. No, they shouldn't. If a marriage cannot work then the partners should get a divorce.
>
> b. Your family is important. You should listen to their advice.
>
> c. I think it is the other way around. After all, there are more divorces in other kinds of marriage than arranged marriages.
>
> d. That is not very respectful. We should respect the beliefs of other people and let them practice their traditions.

Opinion Examples

- Read the opinions and answer the questions.

Opinion A

Track 41

" Everyone should be allowed to choose the person they want to marry. When you marry someone you will spend the rest of your life with that person. Maybe you will raise a family together, too. It's important to know each other well and to love each other before you get married. That way you know that the marriage will be successful. If someone chose your partner for you it's possible you will not like each other. It would be very difficult to live with someone you didn't like. "

Opinion B

Track 42

" I think that arranged marriages are better than choosing your own partner. In an arranged marriage your family makes the decision on who you will marry. That means that your family will like your partner, which does not always happen in other kinds of marriage. Also, they will not choose a bad partner for you. They will think carefully and find someone who is a good match for you. An arranged marriage can also let you focus on other important things like school. Looking for a partner can take a lot of time. For some people it is too difficult. "

1. Please circle the main idea in each opinion.
2. Please underline the supporting ideas in each opinion.
3. What could you say to further support the opinion with which you agree?

Discussion Questions

● **Discuss the questions in groups.**

1. Do you think that couples are happy being in an arranged marriage?

2. Choosing the person you will marry is an important decision. Would it be OK to let your parents make other important decisions for you, like what to study or where to work?

3. What should an arranged couple do if they are not compatible with each other?

4. How would you react if your parents wanted to arrange a marriage for you?

5. How would it feel to be in an arranged marriage?

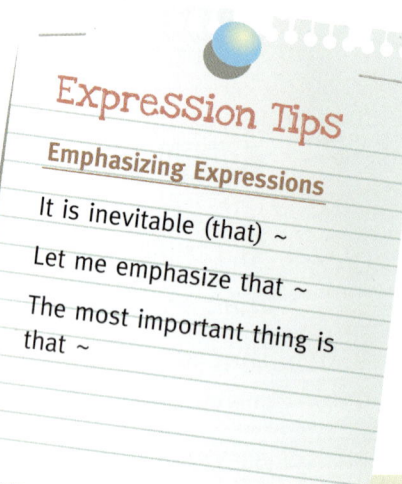

Choose one statement. Debate the statement in groups.
(One group agrees with the statement, the other group disagree with the statement.)

1. You should marry someone because of love, not because your parents tell you to.

2. You should always follow the traditions of your culture and religion.

3. Diversity is bad in a marriage. You should marry someone who is similar to you. It will make the marriage stronger.

UNIT 15 Social Networking

Warm-up

- Social networking websites allow you to create a profile with your personal information. Create your "textbook profile" by providing your personal details below.

1. Name	2. Age
3. ID	4. Password
5. E-mail address	6. Birthday
7. Phone number	8. Hometown
9. Favorite movies	10. Interests
11. Credit card number	

Which should you reveal to others, and which should you hide?

OK to reveal	Should be hidden

- Interview a classmate using the questions below.

  1. Have you ever seen a social networking website? Which ones do you know?
  2. How do you normally keep in touch with your family and friends?

Social Networking

● Read the passage.

Track 43

Social networking has become extremely popular in the last few years. Websites such as *Facebook*, *MySpace*, *Twitter* and *Classmates.com* are frequently visited today. From 2005 to 2009, the number of users on these websites quadrupled. *Facebook* alone reported about 300 million users worldwide in the year 2009.

There are many great things about social networking. For one, it allows you to keep in touch with friends and relatives. It is usually free to use, and can be used anywhere if there is a computer and the Internet. You can use social networks to make new friends, or even find old friends. You can send and receive messages, as well as upload pictures or videos for everyone to see. It also allows you to find people with similar interests. Or you can promote a business or product easily, and to many people.

But social networking can be quite dangerous. There is a strong risk of identity theft. People often post personal information on these sites which anyone can use for illegal purposes. Vulnerable children can be exposed to predators. Computer viruses can be spread through these sites, too. Some people become addicted to social networking, which is unhealthy. Being online all day keeps someone from going out and talking to people in person. Many office-workers and students spend a lot of time on social networking sites instead of working. This decreases productivity at an office and can negatively affect a student's grades.

Comprehension Check Answer the questions.

1. What are the names of some popular social networking websites?
2. How many people used *Facebook* in 2009?
3. How much money does it cost to use a social networking site?
4. Why is there a strong risk of identity theft on these sites?
5. Why are social networking sites bad for office-workers and students?

Vocabulary Check Complete the sentence with a word from the box.

keep in touch	identity theft	upload	site	productivity

1. I hope that you _____ with me after graduation.
2. My sister likes to _____ pictures of her travels for me to see.
3. The business lost a lot of money when its _____ went down.
4. That is my favorite _____ for buying clothes online.
5. Jake was very upset when he became a victim of _____.

Think About It

Think about the advantages and disadvantages of social networking.

Advantages
- Make new friends, or find old friends
-
-
-

Disadvantages
- Vulnerable children can be exposed to predators.
-
-
-

Opinion Practice

● **Practice supporting/refuting the opinions.**

Supporting Opinions

1. You should not post your personal information online… _____
2. You should use social networks if you want to make new friends… _____
3. Social networks can be unhealthy… _____
4. Social networks are a great way for staying in touch with people… _____

> **a.** since you can become addicted and spend too much time using them.
>
> **b.** because anyone can look at it and use it for illegal purposes.
>
> **c.** because you can find people with similar interests as you.
>
> **d.** because they are free and you can send messages from anywhere in the world.

Refuting Opinions

1. Children are too vulnerable to use social networking websites. _____
2. The government should watch social networking websites to look for predators or terrorists. _____
3. If you use a social networking site someone will steal your identity. _____
4. Students should not be allowed to use these sites because they will get bad grades. _____

> **a.** I don't agree. I think this is dangerous. They could spy on innocent people, too.
>
> **b.** That's not true. These sites can help classmates to work together, making their grades better.
>
> **c.** I disagree. I think they are old enough and smart enough to use them. It is a great way for kids to stay in touch with friends.
>
> **d.** That's not necessarily true. This crime happens, but it is rare. Most people have a profile with no problems.

Opinion Examples

● **Read the opinions and answer the questions.**

Opinion A

Track 44

❝ I think that social networking websites are an important communication tool. They are free to use, and can be used all over the world. They let us send messages to family and friends. We can also post pictures and videos of ourselves for others to see. We can even find old friends or make new friends. My mom was able to find old classmates using these sites. She was so happy to see them again after many years of being apart. My dad, too, was able to find other people who shared his interest in model cars. ❞

Opinion B

Track 45

❝ I think that social networking sites are too dangerous, and that the risks are not worth the benefits. Firstly, bad people can see your personal information. They can take it and steal your identity. There is also a risk of people stalking or harassing you on these sites. Some people become addicted to them and spend many hours a day visiting these sites. It is unhealthy, and prevents people from talking to others in real life. Also, there are predators who can take advantage of vulnerable children. ❞

1. Please circle the main idea in each opinion.
2. Please underline the supporting ideas in each opinion.
3. What could you say to further support the opinion with which you agree?

Discussion Questions

● **Discuss the questions in groups.**

1. How much privacy should people have when using a social networking website?

2. What are some ways that we can make social networking websites safer for people to use?

3. Who do you think benefits the most by using social networking websites?

4. How can social networking websites be used by schools to help students?

5. Should the government be allowed to look at our social networking profiles to search for dangerous people?

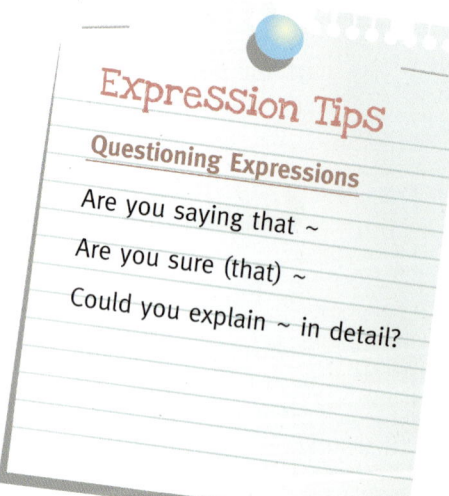

Expression Tips
Questioning Expressions
Are you saying that ~
Are you sure (that) ~
Could you explain ~ in detail?

Choose one statement. Debate the statement in groups.
(One group agrees with the statement, the other group disagree with the statement.)

1. Office workers spend too much time using social networking sites. It causes companies to lose a lot of money. Social networking should be banned in the workplace.

2. Children under the age of 13 should not be allowed to use social networking websites.

3. It is better to socialize with people and make new friends in real life, not on a computer.

UNIT 16 Zoos

Warm-up

- Think of the animals you can see at a zoo. Many have specific needs which the zoo must provide. Fill in the boxes with animal names.

Zoo animals and their needs

A lot of space	Little light	A lot of water
elephants	bats	dolphins

- Interview a classmate using the questions below.

1. What is your favorite animal? Can you see this animal at a zoo?
2. Would you like to work at a zoo? Why or why not?

Zoos

Read the passage.

Zoos date back thousands of years to the ancient Egyptians and Chinese. To them, having exotic animals meant that you were wealthy and powerful. Today, zoos are more concerned with protecting animals and educating the public. But is it right to keep animals at a zoo?

Many believe that all animals have natural rights. It is unethical to take them from the wild for any reason. Many captive animals show signs of distress. Animals are not free to practice their natural hunting and mating practices when they are in captivity. Many animals require special diets to survive, or specific weather conditions. It can be difficult to replicate the needs of these animals, and they may suffer because of this. Animals are also deprived of privacy as people view them all day long.

Proponents of zoos see things differently. Zoos today try very hard to make their facilities better for the animals. Animals are given a proper diet and more space. Many of the animals are rescued from harmful situations. They have been abandoned or injured in the wild, or acquired from a circus. Many of these animals would not survive in the wild, but they are safe in a zoo. Zoos also allow scientists to study animals and learn about them. This can help make new medicines and increase animal health. They even conserve endangered animals by breeding them to increase their population. Zoos also educate the public on how to protect animals and create ecological awareness.

Comprehension Check   Answer the questions.

1. When and where were the first zoos?
2. What are zoos concerned with today?
3. Why are animals in zoos deprived of privacy?
4. How can scientists help all animals by studying the animals at zoos?
5. How can zoos help endangered animals?

Vocabulary Check   Complete the sentence with a word from the box.

| exotic | captivity | abandoned | breed | distress |

1. The prisoners of war were held in _____ for many years.
2. I enjoyed seeing all of the _____ clothes from other countries. They were very colorful and beautiful.
3. The students are showing signs of _____ as they studied for their final exams.
4. A rhinoceros is an endangered animal. We should _____ them so that they do not become extinct.
5. I found a(n) _____ bicycle on the side of the road. No one seemed to own it.

Think About It

Think about the advantages and disadvantages of keeping animals in a zoo.

Advantages
- Many animals have been rescued from harmful situations.
-
-

Disadvantages
- Animals have a right to be free.
-
-

Opinion Practice

● **Practice supporting/refuting the opinions.**

Supporting Opinions

1. Animals should not be kept in zoos... _____
2. We should protect endangered animals... _____
3. Zoos should try to recreate an animal's natural environment as best as possible... _____
4. Schools should take their classes on a trip to the zoo... _____

> a. because if we don't they may become extinct.
> b. because it will help the animal feel comfortable living in a zoo.
> c. because they are wild and should live free in nature.
> d. because it is a great way to learn about different animals.

Refuting Opinions

1. People only go to the zoo for entertainment. _____
2. If zoos did not exist we could not learn about animals. _____
3. We should not have to pay to go to a zoo. It should be free to see these animals. _____
4. Animals at zoos are happy because they are safe from danger. _____

> a. That would be nice, but zoos need money. The entrance fee goes towards feeding the animals and paying the workers.
> b. I disagree. Many people go to learn about different animals. Schools bring students to the zoo, too.
> c. I think they are distressed. They are not free to live a natural life and live in captivity.
> d. That's not true. We can study animals in the wild.

Opinion Examples

● Read the opinions and answer the questions.

Opinion A

Track 47

❝ I don't think that animals should be kept in zoos. Animals have a right to be free. They belong in the wild where they can live naturally. We don't have the right to force animals to live in confinement. I would not want to live in a cage and have people watching me all day. There is no privacy and not enough space to feel comfortable. Many of the animals show signs of distress, so I don't think animals are happy being in a zoo. ❞

Opinion B

Track 48

❝ I think that zoos are very important for helping all animals. Many of the animals in zoos have been abandoned or rescued from dangerous situations. They are not healthy enough to live in the wild, and would die if they were not in zoos. We can learn more about these animals and make new medicines to improve their health. Zoos breed endangered species and reintroduce them into the wild, too. This prevents extinction of endangered species. Zoos also educate people on how we can protect wild animals. ❞

1. Please circle the main idea in each opinion.

2. Please underline the supporting ideas in each opinion.

3. What could you further say to support the opinion with which you agree?

Discussion Questions

● **Discuss the questions in groups.**

1. How could we learn about animals if zoos did not exist?

2. Are animals at zoos happy?

3. Do you think that animals live longer in a zoo or in the wild?

4. How do zoos educate people about animals and influence us to help animals?

5. Do animals have rights? What rights should they have?

Expression Tips

Questioning Expressions

Do you really think (that) ~

Don't you think ~

How can you say (that) ~

Time to Debate

Choose one statement. Debate the statement in groups.
(One group agrees with the statement, the other group disagree with the statement.)

1. Zoos are morally wrong and should be banned.

2. Animals are much safer and healthier at zoos than if they were in the wild.

3. Zoos are not necessary for teaching people about animals.

Single Sex vs. Coed

Warm-up

- Fill in the table with activities you do after school. Then put an "X" in the box if you do it alone, with only your same gender, or with boys and girls.

Activities you do after school	Alone	Same gender	Boys and girls
reading books	X		

Name your three favorite subjects in school.

- Interview a classmate using the questions below.

1. What kind of school do you go to? Is it single sex or coed?
2. Do you have friends of the opposite sex?

Single Sex vs. Coed

🟠 **Read the passage.**

Track 49

Look around your class. Are there boys and girls, or only one sex? Some schools provide a single sex education, meaning they have only girls or only boys. Others allow both genders to attend. There are advantages to both, and it is a personal choice as to which to attend.

Studies show that girls and boys do better academically in single sex schools. There are fewer distractions, especially when it comes to popularity and relationships. Some people are intimidated by the opposite sex. This can make it difficult to participate in class, express opinions and make friends. Girls and boys also mature at different rates and have different needs. It can be easier for the teachers to focus on teaching only one gender at a time. Students even have more freedom to make educational choices. Women won't feel strange for wanting to study stereotypically masculine subjects like math, and vice versa.

Coed schools, on the other hand, are more reflective of society. The real world is not single sex. We must interact with the opposite sex regularly. Research shows that students from single sex schools are more hesitant in expressing their opinions in front of the opposite sex. They also have more trouble forming friendships and relationships with members of the opposite sex. Students from coed schools don't have this problem. There is more diversity in coed schools, too. Their students can learn from working with other people and experiencing different learning styles. For these reasons, many believe that segregation is the wrong way to resolve educational issues.

Comprehension Check Answer the questions.

1. In which kind of schools do students do better academically?
2. What can make it difficult to participate in class, express opinions and make friends?
3. Why is it easier for a teacher to teach in single sex schools?
4. How are coed schools more reflective of society?
5. Which type of school has more diversity?

Vocabulary Check Complete the sentence with a word from the box.

| gender | distraction | intimidated | resolve | stereotypical |

1. It is _____ to say that all men are good at math.
2. We must think of a better way to _____ our educational problems.
3. I was _____ because I thought the other students were smarter than me.
4. Please provide me with your personal information. Include your name, _____, and birth date.
5. A dog ran into my classroom today. It was a big _____ and everyone was surprised.

Think About It

Think about the advantages of going to a single sex school / a coed school.

Advantages of a single sex school
- Teachers can focus on the needs of one gender at a time.
-
-

Advantages of a coed school
- You can experience different learning styles.
-
-

Opinion Practice

- **Practice supporting/refuting the opinions.**

Supporting Opinions

1. Students should go to a school where they feel the most comfortable... _____
2. We should segregate boys and girls... _____
3. If you want to get good grades you should go to a single sex school... _____
4. Coed schools better prepare students for the working world... _____

> a. since when boys and girls are together there are too many distractions.
> b. because if students are uncomfortable they will do poorly in school.
> c. because the world is not single sex and we must interact with the opposite sex regularly.
> d. because students do better academically in single sex schools.

Refuting Opinions

1. Single sex schools don't prepare students for the working world. _____
2. Segregation in schools is good because there are too many distractions in coed schools. _____
3. Boys will be embarrassed if they want to take stereotypically feminine subjects, like literature, in a coed school. _____
4. There is no pressure to be cool in a single sex school. _____

> a. I disagree. I think these students are well prepared academically.
> b. That's not true. There is still a desire to be popular and impress classmates, even if they are the same gender as you.
> c. That's not necessarily true. Many of the world's best writers were men. You should not feel bad doing something you enjoy.
> d. I don't think we should separate people to solve a problem. We should find a new solution.

Opinion Examples

- **Read the opinions and answer the questions.**

Track 50

❝ I think that single sex schools are better than coed schools. I feel really uncomfortable talking with people of the opposite sex. I can't express my opinions in class and I am embarrassed to talk to them. I feel more comfortable talking to others who are the same gender as me. I can focus on my studies without being distracted. And I don't have to worry about trying to impress other people. There is no pressure to be cool or to be in a relationship with other classmates. ❞

Opinion B

Track 51

❝ I think that coed schools are better than single sex schools. Many of my friends are of the opposite sex. I enjoy spending time with them. I also learn many new things from them. The diversity in coed schools is very valuable. It helps prepare me for the real world, too. When I begin to work I will have to interact with many different types of people. A coed education will prepare me for these experiences. A single sex education won't prepare me for this. ❞

1. Please circle the main idea in each opinion.
2. Please underline the supporting ideas in each opinion.
3. What would you say to further support the opinion with which you agree?

Discussion Questions

● **Discuss the questions in groups.**

1. Students from single sex schools sometimes have trouble interacting with members of the opposite sex. Why would they be more hesitant than students from a coed school?

2. Do boys and girls learn differently and/or have different needs at school?

3. Why is diversity a good thing to have in schools?

4. Are coed schools more distracting than single sex schools?

5. Is it wrong to segregate boys and girls into different schools?

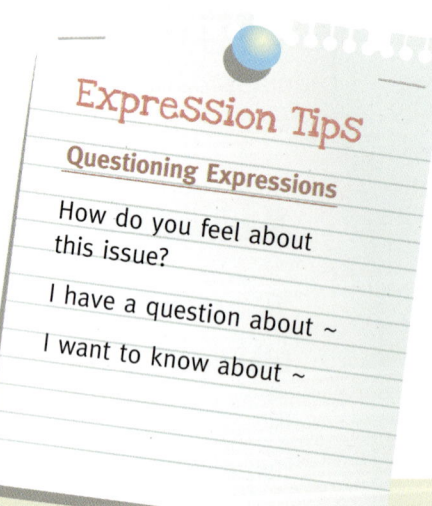

Expression Tips

Questioning Expressions

How do you feel about this issue?

I have a question about ~

I want to know about ~

Choose one statement. Debate the statement in groups.
(One group agrees with the statement, the other group disagree with the statement.)

1. A coed school better prepares its students for life after school.

2. There is too much pressure to be cool and popular at a coed school. Single sex schools don't have this problem.

3. Single sex schools are too competitive academically. You can have more fun at a coed school.

UNIT 18 Space Exploration

Warm-up

● **Find the effect in List B for each cause in List A.**

List A	List B
1. There are too many people on Earth.	a. People on Earth get sick.
2. We run out of natural resources.	b. We discover that aliens exist.
3. We do experiments in space.	c. We build homes on another planet.
4. Astronauts return with a harmful virus.	d. There is not enough money to help poor people.
5. Space exploration becomes too expensive.	e. We find new resources in space.
6. We send radio messages into space.	f. We discover how the universe was created.

● **Interview a classmate using the questions below.**

1. Would you like to be an astronaut and travel in space? Why or why not?
2. Do you think that aliens exist? Could there be life on other planets?

Space Exploration

🔸 Read the passage.

There is something very exciting about going into space. It is fun to explore new places and discover new things. But is space exploration necessary? Should we continue to spend money and resources on exploring space?

There is a great expense involved in sending people into space. The USA alone spends 15.5 billion dollars annually on space exploration. This money could be spent on other important things like helping the poor or improving schools. There is also great risk to human life. Trips to space are very complicated, and mistakes can happen. Astronauts have been hurt and killed on space missions. There is also no guarantee that we find or learn anything important. This whole process could be a waste of time. We may even find something harmful and bring it back to Earth. Others think that the research done in space could be done more easily and cheaply on Earth.

Still, space exploration continues. By doing experiments in space we can learn more about physics, chemistry, biology and other sciences. Scientists can learn about our universe and how it was created. New technologies can be developed to help everyone. Also, Earth's population is increasing while our resources are decreasing. We may need to search for new resources or find a new planet to live on in the future. Putting satellites in space can help us, too. We can get more accurate weather forecasts. Satellites also make communication with phones, radio and the Internet much faster.

Comprehension Check Answer the questions.

1. How much money does the USA spend annually on space exploration?
2. Why is it risky to send humans into space?
3. What can we learn more about by doing experiments in space?
4. Why might we need to search for new resources or a new planet to live on?
5. How do satellites help us?

Vocabulary Check Complete the sentence with a word from the box.

| explore | expense | waste of time | resource | guarantee |

1. I like to go to new countries and _____ the mountains.
2. I did not learn much from my friend. Studying with him was a(n) _____.
3. Oil is a natural _____ that many people fight over.
4. Can you _____ that this computer is better than the other computer?
5. Going to university can be a great _____ for many people.

Think About It

Think about the advantages and disadvantages of space exploration.

Advantages
- We can find new resources and planets.
-
-

Disadvantages
- The money spent could be used on other important things.
-
-

Opinion Practice

- **Practice supporting/refuting the opinions.**

Supporting Opinions

1. We should not send humans into space... _____
2. We should use robots to explore space... _____
3. We should spend our money and resources helping people on Earth... _____
4. Scientists should do their experiments on Earth... _____

> a. because there is the risk that they could die.
>
> b. because they can find out information without risking human lives.
>
> c. because there are many people on Earth who need help. There is no guarantee that space exploration can help us.
>
> d. since we can still explore space without risking human lives.

Refuting Opinions

1. We can only learn about the universe by doing experiments in space. _____
2. If we go into space we will return with a new, dangerous disease. _____
3. Space exploration should be banned because it is a waste of money. _____
4. We should use robots instead of astronauts to help save lives. _____

> a. That's not necessarily true. There have been many missions into space and so far they have returned with nothing harmful.
>
> b. That's not true. We can learn many things by exploring space. We should continue to learn more about the universe.
>
> c. That may be true; however, they will be very expensive to make and difficult to control. It's better to have real people on missions.
>
> d. I disagree. We can do tests on Earth to help us learn about space. It will be cheaper and faster, too.

Opinion Examples

Read the opinions and answer the questions.

Track 53

❝ We should spend our time and money on important issues instead of exploring space. Sending people to space costs a lot of money. There is no guarantee that it will even help us. In the meantime, there are many problems in society which need to be fixed. We can spend that money improving schools and giving teachers more money. We can give money to poor people who need food and safe homes. There are many ways that this money can help all people. ❞

Opinion B

Track 54

❝ We should continue to spend money on missions to space. In the future we may run out of natural resources. We may need to find new minerals, or even a new planet to live on. If we do not explore space now this will not be possible in the future. There are also many scientific benefits. We can learn more about physics, chemistry and biology. We can develop new technologies to make life on Earth easier. Space exploration will make our lives in the future better. ❞

1. Please circle the main idea in each opinion.
2. Please underline the supporting ideas in each opinion.
3. What would you say to further support the opinion with which you agree?

Discussion Questions

● **Discuss the questions in groups.**

1. What is the most important thing we can learn from space exploration?

2. If you could, would you go to space as a tourist? Why or why not?

3. Will we ever build homes on the moon or another planet?

4. Imagine you could take the money spent on space missions and use it to help people. What is the most important issue on Earth that you think needs help?

5. Is it important to learn about how the universe began? Why or why not?

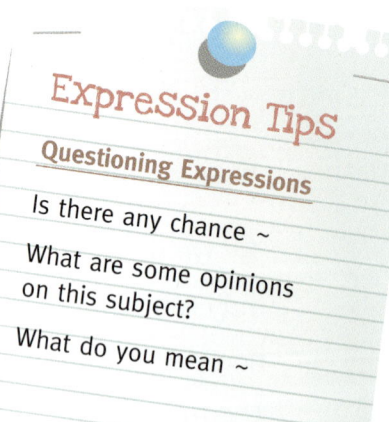

Expression Tips
Questioning Expressions
Is there any chance ~
What are some opinions on this subject?
What do you mean ~

Choose one statement. Debate the statement in groups.
(One group agrees with the statement, the other group disagrees with the statement.)

1. We should not send humans into space. It is too dangerous.

2. Mars is the closest planet to Earth. We should do experiments to see if we could live on Mars in the future.

3. The scientific profit to humans is not worth the time and money spent on space exploration.

UNIT 19
Free Trade Agreements (FTAs)

ED2-19
MP3

Warm-up

● **Check the tags on your clothes and find where they were made.**

Article of clothing (shirt, pants, hat, shoes, etc.)	Country

● **Interview a classmate using the questions below.**

1. Do you like the goods from other countries? Which goods do you like?
2. Do you ever buy products that are made in your home country? What do you buy?

Free Trade Agreements (FTAs)

● Read the passage.

Track 55

Free trade agreements, or FTAs, are policies between two or more nations. They allow countries to trade goods with each other with little or no government interference. Hundreds of these agreements exist all over the world. It is important to know if FTAs are helpful, or hurtful to us all.

These agreements let exporters send goods to another country without paying tariffs. This allows companies to save money and sell their goods at lower prices. Consumers are given a greater variety of goods and services at a decreased price. Increased trading between countries promotes competition between similar companies. These companies will be forced to innovate and get better to keep making money. This keeps the quality of goods high. It also promotes peace, as countries work together to help each other.

Opponents worry that FTAs will make the demand for domestic products decrease. People will buy cheaper imports from other countries. Domestic businesses will suffer and lose money, and people will lose their jobs. The government loses money, too, as it does not get tariff money from imports anymore. Human rights activists worry about the rights of workers in other countries. Poor countries sometimes treat their workers badly. They work long hours for little money. Businesses give their jobs to these workers because it is an easy way to save money. They produce goods at the lowest possible price, even if workers rights and the environment are sacrificed.

Comprehension Check — Answer the questions.

1. What do FTAs allow countries to do?
2. How do FTAs benefit consumers?
3. What do FTAs allow exporters to do?
4. How do FTAs promote peace?
5. Why do human rights activists worry about FTAs?

Vocabulary Check — Complete the sentence with a word from the box.

| domestic | tariff | consumers | exporters | imports |

1. _____ like to buy high quality goods at a cheap price.
2. I think that it is better to buy _____ goods instead of buying them from foreign countries.
3. I like that store. It has many products which are _____ as well as many domestic choices.
4. We do not have a free trade agreement with that country. They must pay a(n) _____ if they want to sell their goods here.
5. The _____ made a lot of money selling their products in other countries.

Think About It

Think about the advantages and disadvantages of FTAs.

Advantages
- Companies save money because they don't pay tariffs.
-
-

Disadvantages
- It decreases the demand for domestic products.
-
-

Opinion Practice

● **Practice supporting/refuting the opinions.**

Supporting Opinions

1. We should only buy domestic products... _____
2. We should work together with other countries... _____
3. Consumers should support FTAs... _____
4. Companies should continue to innovate... _____

> a. because it will allow them to make more money.
>
> b. since it allows them to have a greater variety of goods at a decreased price.
>
> c. because it helps to promote peace between nations.
>
> d. because it will support our economy and prevent us from sending our money to other countries.

Refuting Opinions

1. FTAs are bad because people might lose their jobs. _____
2. We should ban FTAs because it allows rich countries to take advantage of workers in poor countries. _____
3. Domestic products are better than foreign products. _____
4. The government should never interfere with the trading of goods between countries. _____

> a. That may be true, but more jobs will be created in other countries.
>
> b. I disagree. FTAs may actually help these people get better working conditions and more money.
>
> c. That's not necessarily true. We can import high quality goods which are better than ones made domestically.
>
> d. I don't agree with that. It is important for the people in power to have knowledge of the imports and exports of a country.

Opinion Examples

- Read the opinions and answer the questions.

Opinion A

Track 56

" I think that FTAs are bad for the rights of workers. They allow rich companies to buy goods from poor countries. Companies will not have to make their goods with domestic workers who get a good salary. They can import their goods from poor countries that hire workers for little money. These workers often work long hours in bad working conditions. It is sometimes cheaper for companies to buy imports than to pay people to make them. This causes domestic workers to lose their jobs, too. "

Opinion B

Track 57

" I think that FTAs help businesses and workers around the world. They promote trade between companies in different countries. This allows a company to make more money. They will then have more money to pay their workers. It can also help create more jobs. People will be needed to make more of the goods and to transport them around the world. In the end, FTAs will make more jobs for people around the world. Workers will also save money because they can buy goods at a cheap price in a store. "

1. Please circle the main idea in each opinion.
2. Please underline the supporting ideas in each opinion.
3. What would you say to further support the opinion with which you agree?

Discussion Questions

● **Discuss the questions in groups.**

1. Why is it important to support domestic businesses?

2. How do FTAs affect your everyday life?

3. What are some reasons that it is bad that governments lose money by not collecting tariffs in FTAs?

4. Do FTAs help or hurt poor countries?

5. How can FTAs help your country?

Choose one statement. Debate the statement in groups.
(One group agrees with the statement, the other group disagrees with the statement.)

1. FTAs are a good idea to help people and countries.

2. It is better to pay more money for a domestic good than to buy an imported good for less money.

3. FTAs may cause countries to sacrifice the environment or worker's rights to compete with other businesses.

UNIT 20 Human Nature... Good or Evil?

ED2-20
MP3

Warm-up

● **Brian is a good boy and Gary is a bad boy. Match the actions in the box with each boy.**

Good vs. Bad

Brian	Gary

comforts a sad friend   donates to charity   cheats on tests
fights with classmates   lies to parents   steals from stores
makes fun of classmates   loves his parents   volunteers at school
helps friends with homework

● **Interview a classmate using the questions below.**

1. What are some good things that you have done for others?
2. Have you ever done any bad things in your life? What are some bad things you have done?

Human Nature... Good or Evil?

🟠 **Read the passage.**

Track 58

Are humans good or evil? This is one of the most difficult and complex questions in history. Philosophers have been debating it for years, and today the answer is still not certain.

It can be difficult to say that all humans are good. If you read the news, it is easy to see that bad things happen every day. People kill each other, fight, and steal. Prisons are full of criminals who have committed evil or unlawful actions. We have wars which destroy families and breed hate between countries. Some people are very rich while others live in extreme poverty. Even young children do bad things like lie to their parents or cheat in school.

But there is plenty of evidence to suggest that humans are good, not evil. Parents take care of and love their children. Volunteer work is done all over the world to help underprivileged people. People donate their money to charities which help people, animals, and groups in need. Human kindness can be seen in everyday activities, too. Friends support and make each other feel good. They may help you study for a test or talk to you when you are feeling sad. If you drop money on the floor a stranger may even pick it up and return it to you.

As you can see, this is not an easy question to answer. Based on your experiences, what do you think is the inherent nature of humans... good or evil?

Comprehension Check — Answer the questions.

1. Do philosophers today know if humans are good or evil?
2. Why can it be difficult to say that all humans are good?
3. What do wars do to people?
4. Why do people donate money to charities?
5. How can friends help each other?

Vocabulary Check — Complete the sentence with a word from the box.

| stranger | inherent | donate | certain | underprivileged |

1. I am not _____ that this is the correct answer to the question.
2. I would like to _____ my old clothes to charity.
3. I believe that the _____ nature of humans is to be good because all of the people I know are good.
4. It is very sad to see the way that _____ people live in poor countries.
5. I don't know him. He is a(n) _____ to me.

Think About It

Think about the evidence to suggest that humans are good or evil.

Proof that humans are good
- Parents take care of and love their children.
-
-

Proof that humans are evil
- People kill each other.
-
-

Opinion Practice

- **Practice supporting/refuting the opinions.**

    Supporting Opinions

    1. We should stop fighting wars... _____
    2. You should not lie to others... _____
    3. People are inherently evil... _____
    4. We should donate money to charities... _____

    > a. because it is good to be honest with people.
    > b. because I see so many bad things in the news every day.
    > c. because helping people who are poorer than you is the right thing to do.
    > d. because they are evil and breed hate between people.

    Refuting Opinions

    1. When you donate money you should get something in return. _____
    2. All people are born with the ability to do evil and learn to be good from their parents. _____
    3. All evil people should go to prison. _____
    4. Committing murder is always an evil act. _____

    > a. That's not necessarily true. You can be evil but not commit a crime or break the laws of society.
    > b. I think the opposite is true. Babies are born good and innocent. They learn about evil from other people.
    > c. That's very greedy. You should give because it is good to help others.
    > d. I don't think this is always true. It is not evil to kill someone in self defense.

Opinion Examples

- Read the opinions and answer the questions.

Opinion A

Track 59

" I think that humans are inherently good. When I look around, I see people doing good things every day. My family members are all good people. They love me and support me when I need them. My friends, too, help me study and be better at sports. I even see strangers helping each other. They never ask for anything in return. They do these things because they are good people and because it is the right thing to do. "

Opinion B

Track 60

" I think that humans are inherently evil. When I see the news I hear about all of the bad things that happened in the world every day. Countries fight each other in wars. People kill each other over silly things like money. There are also so many rich people living right next to people who live in poverty. Even my classmates make fun of each other and are mean to each other. If everyone was good we would not have these problems; therefore, people are evil. "

1. Please circle the main idea in each opinion.
2. Please underline the supporting ideas in each opinion.
3. What would you say to further support the opinion with which you agree?

Discussion Questions

● **Discuss the questions in groups.**

1. Can people be both good and evil at the same time, or only one or the other?
2. Why do people do evil things?
3. Who decides what is good and what is evil?
4. Can a baby have the ability to do evil things?
5. What does it mean to be a good person?

Expression Tips

Questioning Expressions

What's your opinion on this?

Why do you think (that) ~

Choose one statement. Debate the statement in groups.
(One group agrees with the statement, the other group disagrees with the statement.)

1. Animals have the ability to be good or evil, just like humans.
2. People are born inherently good, and learn about evil from society and other people.
3. Fighting is not always evil. Sometimes it is a good thing to fight other people.